Who's Pulling Your Strings?

Other books by Dr. Harriet Braiker

The September 11 Syndrome
The Disease to Please
Lethal Lovers and Poisonous People
Getting Up When You're Feeling Down
The Type E Woman

Who's Pulling Your Strings?

How to Break the Cycle
of Manipulation and Regain
Control of Your Life

Harriet B. Braiker, Ph.D.

McGraw-Hill

New York   Chicago   San Francisco   Lisbon   London
Madrid   Mexico City   Milan   New Delhi   San Juan
Seoul   Singapore   Sydney   Toronto

The McGraw·Hill Companies

Library of Congress Cataloging-in-Publication Data

Braiker, Harriet B.
  Who's pulling your strings?: how to break the cycle of manipulation
and regain control of your life/by Harriet B. Braiker
    p. cm.
Includes bibliographical references and index.
  ISBN 0-07-140278-0 (alk. paper)
  1. Manipulative behavior. 2. Control (Psychology) I. Title.
  BF632.5B69 2003
  158.2--dc21   2003008602

1 2 3 4 5 6 7 8 9 0 /DOC/DOC/ 09876543

ISBN 0-07-140278-0

This publication is designed to provide accurate and authoritative information in regard to the subject matter covered. It is sold with the understanding that the publisher is not engaged in rendering legal, accounting, or other professional service. If legal advice or other expert assistance is required, the services of a competent professional person should be sought.

—From a declaration of principles jointly adopted by a committee of the American Bar Association and a committee of publishers.

McGraw-Hill books are available at special quantity discounts to use as premiums and sales promotions, or for use in corporate training programs. For more information, please write to the Director of Special Sales, Professional Publishing, McGraw-Hill, Two Penn Plaza, New York, NY 10121-2298. Or contact your local bookstore.

This book is printed on recycled, acid-free paper containing a minimum of 50% recycled, de-inked fiber.

For Steven and Amanda
It's all about them.

Contents

Introduction

THROUGHOUT my career I have been interested in the psychological problems that men and women develop as a result of their good—but often misguided—intentions. In the mid-1980s, just as the full thrust of the women's movement was beginning to alter the American labor force and the fabric of American life, I wrote *The Type E Woman: How to Overcome the Stress of Being Everything to Everybody*. That book compared and contrasted the different types of stresses of men and women. Specifically, it examined the continuing stress cycles created by women's flawed attempts to "have it all" by trying to meet everyone else's needs at the expense of their own health and welfare.

For nearly 20 years now, high-achieving women across the United States and, indeed, the world over have identified with the Type E concept. They have populated my clinical practice, retained me to consult in their businesses, invited me to give keynote speeches, and formed a receptive and gracious audience for my radio and television appearances.

No matter how powerful or successful, Type E women talk to me about how their desire to make others happy sets them up to be victims in damaging manipulative relationships.

I revisited the topic of people-pleasing, twenty-first century style, just a few years ago in another book called *The Disease to Please: Curing the People-Pleasing Syndrome.* This time, aided by the Internet, I created a Web site—*www.DiseaseTo-Please.com*—for readers to communicate with me as well as with other people-pleasers so that they could benefit from an online supportive community.

Since publication of *The Disease to Please* in 2001, I have received a continuous stream of e-mails and messages on the Web site's guest book from *both* women and men who identify with the problem. The theme of these messages is consistent: People-pleasers' nice intentions make them an easy mark for manipulators. And the victim status they adopt when manipulators wrest away their freedom, self-direction, and sense of personal control creates deeper and more damaging emotional problems.

The message to me came loud and clear: My readers could really use a good self-help book that cuts through the fog of confusion that manipulation produces. They need to better understand why, how, when, and by whom they get manipulated. *Most important, of course, they need to know what they can do to stop it.*

However, make no mistake, people-pleasers are by no means the only ones vulnerable to manipulation. Nearly 30 years of practice as a clinical psychologist and management consultant have driven that point home to me. I have witnessed the painful, disruptive, and disabling effects of manipulation on patients and clients from varied backgrounds, with disparate personalities, of wide age ranges, and all levels of economic, educational, and social status.

Some people *are* easier targets than others, but nobody is completely invulnerable to skilled manipulators. I have worked with patients and corporate clients who never felt the need to speak to a psychologist until they found themselves under someone's thumb—unable to extricate themselves from a manipulative spouse, a controlling boss, an ambitious subordinate, a back-stabbing competitive coworker, a guilt-inducing mother, or an insecure friend. The list of manipulators goes on and on.

My own experience with manipulative relationships extends well beyond a merely professional interest. I know firsthand the toll on self-esteem, happiness, and emotional and physical health that manipulation exacts. I have been entangled in the insidious web of coercive, manipulative control. I never want to go there again.

In the interest of self-protection, as well as the welfare of those who seek my professional help, I have worked for many years to develop tactics and strategies to resist manipulation. I have written *Who's Pulling Your Strings?* in order to share those skills with a wide audience. My goal, simply, is to help readers break the shackles of manipulation and reclaim control over their own lives.

There are a few important caveats about the audience for this book. *Who's Pulling Your Strings?* is about emotional or psychological manipulation. It is not intended to apply to relationships in which physical violence—or the threat of physical violence—is used as a means of control.

If you are the victim of a physically abusive relationship, you do not have the luxury to read this book. Not now. You need to take urgent steps to protect yourself and others by putting as much physical and psychological distance as possible between you and the person who has been abusing you.

Neither is this book intended for people being manipulated by someone who abuses alcohol and/or drugs. Alcoholics, addicts, and substance abusers are quite literally not in their right minds by virtue of the intoxicants they ingest. You simply cannot deal effectively with an abuser until he or she gets the substance-abuse problem under control. As long as substance abusers keep drinking or using, your problems with them will continue. Manipulation is a core symptom of their illness; you need to be part of the solution, not part of the problem.

Finally, this book is not intended for those being pressured or coerced into illegal activities. Whether it is a corrupt boss at work who wants you to "cook the books," a boyfriend or girlfriend who intends to lie and defraud others and wants you to swear to it, or any other person who is pushing you to cross the line of criminal behavior, you need to get away from the relationship and away from the manipulator *immediately.* There is no room here for negotiation.

Barring these exceptions, this book is for you. How do I know? I have yet to meet anyone who has *not* been manipulated by someone at some point in his or her life. So everyone can benefit from learning how to resist manipulation. If you are the victim or target of a manipulative relationship right now, take comfort in knowing that you are not alone. Millions of people share the feelings that manipulation produces—the impotent sense that there is nothing you can do to interrupt the toxic cycle or to limit the damage.

This is just how a manipulator wants you to feel.

My fervent hope is that this book will shed new light on your problem and change your feelings of helplessness, confusion, and loss of control. If we succeed together, you will have a great answer the next time someone asks you, "Who's pulling your strings?" You can look them dead in the eye and say, "Nobody but me."

1

An Overview
of Manipulation

Have you ever felt as though someone is pulling your strings—making you do things you would rather not or stopping you from doing things you would prefer to continue? Have you tried to untangle the strings only to find that you become more entrapped with each futile struggle?

Manipulation respects no relationship boundaries. It can invade your most intimate personal relationships with your spouse or lover. It can happen at work—with peers and non-peers alike. Manipulative relationships occur in families, organizations, friendships, professional relationships, and even at churches, synagogues, mosques, or other places of worship.

There are no age limitations or gender preferences. Men *and* women of all ages and sexual orientations can be manipulative and manipulated. And whenever life transitions—positive or negative—take place with their inevitable stress, uncertainty, and anxiety, the red carpet is unfurled for manipulation.

Ironically, manipulation takes particular hold in those relationships where you have the most to gain and/or the most to lose. These include your most significant bonds—your family, marriage, romantic partner, coworkers, friends, even your mentors and advisors.

If someone is pulling your strings, then I have written this book for you.

If you are the victim—or former victim—of manipulation, you very likely feel confused, resentful, frustrated, helpless, stuck, and/or pretty angry. You are also likely to feel guilty, anxious, and depressed, especially if the manipulation has gone on for a long time.

You probably want to know why and how you became ensnared in such a maddening no-win relationship so that it will not happen to you again. Most important, you want to know—you *need* to know—how to stop being manipulated. This book will answer your questions.

Control and Countercontrol

When you participate in a manipulative relationship, you unwittingly collude with the person who seeks to control you. Every time you comply, capitulate, cave in, or otherwise satisfy your manipulator's wishes and purposes, you reinforce the toxic cycle that is compromising your self-esteem, co-opting your values, and corroding your emotional wiring.

Being manipulated is a highly stressful experience. It is unpleasant, demeaning, and disturbing. And it is harmful to your physical health, too—literally.

I wrote this book for people who are targeted, exploited, and controlled by manipulators. I did not write this book to enlighten manipulators about the unfairness of their tactics and purposes. Nor do I expect to change the minds or methods of manipulative people by appealing to them directly. These would be futile exercises.

Instead, I wrote this book to make you and other victims of manipulation aware of your countercontrol. And I intend to empower you to use that countercontrol. I realize that your participation in the manipulation probably has made you feel quite powerless. This is what the manipulator wants you to believe. However, the truth is that you hold the key to either making the manipulator successful or foiling his or her efforts.

Manipulation is used because *it works*. As long as you allow a manipulator to exploit and control you, he or she will continue to manipulate. However, if you make the manipulation ineffective by *changing your behavior*, the manipulator will be forced to change tactics or to seek an easier target elsewhere.

You are not likely to change a manipulator by pointing out that her tactics are unfair or that you feel unhappy with the way the relationship is going. To put it bluntly, manipulators do not care about your feelings. They are out to serve one purpose: to advance their own interests and goals, frequently at your expense. If you benefit from a manipulative relationship, it is merely accidental.

You can, however, exercise countercontrol to change the power balance of the relationship. When you stop rewarding manipulative tactics by ceasing to cooperate, comply, please, acquiesce, apologize, or respond to intimidation or threats, you will *unilaterally* alter the nature of the manipulative relationship. Then you can stop or at least begin to reverse the emotional havoc that the relationship has wreaked.

Manipulation versus Influence

To manipulate, according to Webster's, is "to control or play upon by artful, unfair, or insidious means, especially to one's own advantage; to change by artful or unfair means to serve one's purposes."

For the purposes of this book, as well as your own self-protection, you should assume that being on the receiving end of manipulation is necessarily a negative, harmful experience. Manipulation reinforces dependency, helplessness, and victimization. In turn, these rigid roles constrict the relationship's capacity to function or grow normally in a healthy and balanced way. Under the burdensome weight of manipulation, relationships stagnate into a highly lopsided power imbalance.

As long as the manipulation persists, the manipulator grows seemingly stronger and bolder in his tactics, although insecurity and fears may lie within. And the victim grows weaker and ever more compliant, even as hostility grows within.

Manipulation is different from—and should not be confused with—legitimate, direct, above-board influence. We all engage in attempts to influence others. In some relationships, such as parent-child, teacher-student, and therapist-patient bonds, attempted influence in the service of the target's best interests and needs is central to the definition of roles.

Healthy, appropriate influence generally is shaped by a process of reward. It is guided by open, honest, and direct communication. Strategies of threats and coercion are not used. The agenda or purpose of the influence is defined and made public to the participants.

In contrast, manipulation thrives in an atmosphere of indirect, devious, and even deceptive communication. Agendas frequently are hidden and purposes disguised. Threats, intimidation, and coercion are preferred tactics. Manipulators seek the opportunity to ensnare and cntrap their victims. They often proceed in subtle, devious, or covert ways so that the manipulative character of the relationship is well established long before its true nature becomes apparent to the victim.

Some manipulators are fully conscious and intentional about their actions. They are skilled at coercion and control and take pride in their ability to bend others' wills to suit their purposes. Other manipulative people, however, operate from less conscious or intentional motives. These manipulators may act out of their own fear, insecurity, or other emotional drives and may not be fully aware of the manipulative impact of their actions. Still, they make the basic connection between their tactics—what they do to exert pressure on their target— and the compliance they seek. And they continue to use coercive tactics to advance their own interests.

Whether their manipulation is intentional or unintentional, once rewarded, manipulators exert the same negative impact on their victims. In both cases, the victim's compliance or capitulation rewards the manipulator's efforts and fuels the cycle of ongoing coercion and control.

The Book's Three Purposes

The first purpose of this book is to help you decode and better understand how manipulation works. As you become more knowledgeable about the motives and methods of manipulators, you will become more adept at spotting potential manipulators in your midst and avoiding them before they pull you into their web of control.

You will better understand your role as an unwitting collaborator with those who seek to manipulate you for their personal gain, frequently at the expense of your self-interests. And you will identify aspects of your personality and mind-set that make you particularly vulnerable to manipulation.

Second, the book will help you strengthen those areas of your personality that set you up as a soft target or a "mark" for manipulation. By hardening yourself as a target and by developing a keen awareness of the motives and methods of manipulators, you will be less vulnerable to manipulative control now and in the future.

Third, and most important, this book will teach you the necessary resistance tactics to help you break free of manipulation. The resistance tactics can be adapted to any manipulative relationship. With the knowledge of what is possible, you can choose your battles and decide how far to go and with whom.

You also will face head-on the difficult but essential question of when to stay and when to leave—when to put your efforts toward modifying the relationship dynamic by changing your own behavior first and when to put your efforts toward separating yourself from the manipulative relationship and the manipulator altogether.

Who Is Vulnerable to Manipulation?

The short answer is: everybody. The longer answer is that some people are more vulnerable than others. These easy marks or soft targets are like catnip to manipulators. Susceptible marks broadcast—albeit inadvertently—their vulnerability in the habits and mind-sets they display to others. Picking up the cues, manipulators are drawn to these soft areas or "buttons" in their target's personality and then proceed to push with impunity.

In Chapter 3 you will have an opportunity to assess your own vulnerability to manipulation. First, though, I would like to take you through five case studies of manipulation to put some human faces and warm-blooded feelings on the cold calculus of manipulation.

2

Manipulation in Five Acts

MANIPULATION COMES in many forms and guises. If the written case studies of all the patients I have treated in my career who were involved in manipulative relationships were placed end to end, they would number in the hundreds—if not thousands—of pages, far too many for one book. For our purposes, I have chosen five stories that are representative of the coercive control and helplessness that manipulation creates.

In the brief case studies that follow, you will meet some of my patients and some of the people in their lives—spouses, romantic partners, parents, siblings, coworkers, and so on. And you will be introduced to the manipulative situations they faced. If you are now or have ever been in a manipulative relationship, you may very well recognize or identify with some of these people and their situations that may seem disturbingly familiar. Keep these case studies in mind as you read through this book. I will be referring back to many of these examples to illustrate key points about manipulation as we proceed.

As you learn about the dynamics of manipulation and the resistance tactics that can effectively derail the process, think about how you would handle the dilemmas in which my patients found themselves. Later, we will revisit these case studies and find out how each was resolved.

Act One: A Tale of Two Cindys

Bob is a very successful physician in Beverly Hills, California. He is often invited to deliver speeches or appear on distinguished panels at medical conferences around the country. On one of his trips to New York City, he met Cindy, whose job it was to coordinate and produce medical conferences for large pharmaceutical companies, universities, and other clients. Bob and Cindy were attracted to each other immediately and soon began an intense romance.

It had both the excitement and difficulties that typify long-distance relationships, given his home and medical practice on the West Coast and her home and base of operations on the East Coast. As the relationship grew, Bob would find himself flying to New York almost weekly for passionate but all-too-brief weekends.

When he first came to see me, I asked Bob what had initially attracted him to Cindy. He told me, without hesitation, that he loved her confidence. She was beautiful, well poised, self-assured, a great conversationalist, and a terrific lover. But above all, he prized her seeming independence. She had built a successful career, and from his perspective as a participant at many of the medical conferences she orchestrated, Cindy seemed supremely competent at her job, too.

After 3 months of living apart, Bob and Cindy decided that the long-distance part of the relationship was becoming too difficult for them both, and they discussed living together and eventually getting married. There was little debate about logistics. They agreed that it would be both unwise and impractical for Bob to give up his thriving medical practice and start over from scratch in New York. Therefore, Cindy happily volunteered to move west. Within a month of their decision, Cindy packed up and moved in with Bob in his plush West Los Angeles home.

At first it was bliss for them both. Cindy doted on Bob, always making herself available to him. She loved cooking for him and fussing over him, and Bob loved the attention, which he tried to reciprocate in kind.

Then one day a couple of weeks into the new setup, Bob announced that he had made plans to play tennis with some of his friends the coming Saturday. Cindy was not happy about that at all. Her reaction took Bob by surprise.

She pouted and complained that she was being "abandoned" after she had "given up everything" to move to California. She did not know anyone in California, and "what was she supposed to do while he was out all day," and so on along that refrain.

Just like that, Cindy seemed entirely different to Bob. The independent, self-confident New Yorker now looked more like a needy, dependent woman.

This was a side of Cindy Bob had never seen before—and one that he did not like. But Cindy's mood rebounded after Bob promised to hurry back to her as soon as the game was over, forfeiting his plans to have lunch with his friends.

For a while, it seemed, the "old" Cindy was back.

However, the tennis game incident was just the beginning. Each time Bob wanted or needed to go somewhere alone, Cindy's complaints increased. At first she tried pouting, sulking, crying, the silent treatment, playing the martyr, and withholding sex as ways to pressure and punish Bob. Often she succeeded in manipulating him into changing his plans or, occasionally, inviting her to come along. She was very adept at making him feel guilty for leaving her alone.

Over time, her sulking gave way to angry outbursts and screaming fits. Since Bob hated fighting and emotional chaos, he was readily manipulated. He canceled plans, turned down invitations for tennis and golf, and shortened his workouts at the gym. Her angry outbursts so unnerved Bob that he found himself quickly placating her whenever she started to scream at him. He was looking for a way to shut off "the pain" as quickly as possible. Cindy, for her part, saw how effective a raised voice could be as a potent weapon in her arsenal and did not hesitate to pull it out with alarming frequency. Eventually, if he only thought Cindy's anger was about to erupt, he capitulated almost immediately to whatever she asked.

Sometimes, after he apologized and promised never to "abandon" her, the "old" Cindy would return, at least for a short time. But Bob was troubled by the pattern that had developed. Most of all, he was bothered by his own behavior. He did not respect men who were manipulated by women. The "new" Cindy was weighing him down with her clingy, unstable behavior. She was tearful or raging angry whenever he tried to make plans with his male friends. Worse, Cindy even started punishing Bob with the silent treatment or by withholding sex whenever he was "on call" for the weekend.

Bob so dreaded Cindy's punishing emotional meltdowns that he developed sharp stomach pains whenever he made plans to play tennis or golf with his friends. Cindy passed no opportunity to remind Bob of all that she had given up to move to California. He was disappointed with her lack of effort to make new friends or find something worthwhile to do, but she was expert at pulling his guilt strings. After all, he reasoned, how could he abandon her after the sacrifices she had made for him?

He began buying her expensive presents to ease his conscience, a behavior she actively encouraged. If Bob took a call from one of his friends at home, he could sense Cindy beginning to pout, and his stomach tensed up with pain in anticipation of the scene that was sure to ensue.

Bob felt as though he lived with two Cindys—the confident, supportive woman he had fallen in love with only 6 months ago and the one that used every emotional ploy to get him to bend to her will. The bigger problem was that he did not like or respect the "new" Bob that the second Cindy seemed to bring out.

Six months after Cindy moved in with him, Bob came to see me. Bob's physician referred him to me after tactfully suggesting that Bob's stomach pains were likely the result of having "two" women in his life.

Act Two: Dinner at Mom's

Jim and Sally originally came to see me for couples' therapy. They had been in a long-term relationship and wanted to work out some relatively minor issues before getting married. The therapy was successful, and the wedding took place.

A little more than 1 year later, I was a bit surprised to find their names on my appointment schedule again. This time there were family problems.

Sally came from a small family. There were her parents and one sister, Susie. Susie was married and had two small children.

Bob's family was considerably larger. Besides his parents, he had four siblings—two brothers and two sisters—all of whom were married and had a slew of kids among them.

The new problem focused on Sally's mom, Martha, who always made Friday night dinner for the family—meaning Susie, her husband and two kids, and of course, Sally. When Sally married Jim, Martha expected Sally and Jim for dinner every Friday night, too. As she had done all her life, Sally complied with her mother's desires.

After several months of regular Friday night dinners at Martha's, however, Sally's husband, Jim, expressed a desire to spend some Friday nights with his own family. Sally felt that Jim had a valid point, so she told her mom one day that they would not be over for dinner on the next Friday night. Her mom did not take the news well.

She asked incredulously how Sally could break with this long-standing Friday night tradition. Sally tried to explain that Jim had a right to spend time with his family, too. But in no time Sally felt the familiar guilt for having upset her mother. Martha sobbed softly that Sally would be breaking her father's heart and hurting her sister if she and Jim broke ranks and went elsewhere on Fridays. "We're just a small family, and if you don't come, then we'll feel so lonely. Your sister won't get a chance to see you either, and you know how close you two are and how much she and her kids look forward each week to seeing you."

Sally, now riddled with guilt, said that the plans with Jim's parents for the following week had already been made and could not be changed. She apologized profusely, asking her mother to forgive her just this one time. During that long week, however, Sally got the cold chill from her mother. The daily mother-to-daughter calls ceased. When Sally called her mother, she could only reach the answering machine. And despite her messages, the calls were not returned. When Sally finally managed to get her mother on the phone, she received curt, monosyllabic responses. Sally was getting frostbite.

By Friday morning, Sally caved in under the heavy burden of guilt. She pled with Jim to cancel with his parents and to go to her mother's house that night for dinner. Otherwise, she feared, her mother might never speak to her again. "The silent treatment," she said, "is unbearable." Jim acceded because he could not stand to see Sally in such distress. But his resentment toward Martha grew.

Sally and Jim resumed their previous pattern of Fridays at Martha's. However, as weeks went by, Jim became ever more resentful of the manipulation of his wife—and his own manipulation, too, he reminded himself—by his mother-in-law. He would come to dinner on Fridays, but his mood was surly. He withdrew and did not participate in conversations.

To Sally, things had gone from bad to worse. Now she felt as though her mother *and* her husband were manipulating her at the same time. She was between a rock and a hard place—caught between Jim's sulking, punishing behavior and her mother's masterful guilt induction.

Sally even tried asking Martha to invite Jim's family to Friday night dinners, too. Her mother said that she would love to but that "there's so many of them and we have only a small dining room table in the apartment." Sally offered to make dinner some Friday nights and invite both families. But Martha rejected the idea out of hand because "it just wouldn't be the same." Besides, she did not want to "break the tradition."

Jim, in the meanwhile, was starting to catch heat from his side of the family. While they did not have a Friday night tradition as strong as Martha's, they did like to get together on Friday, have a casual dinner, and just have fun. Worse, some of his family began to feel that maybe Sally did not like them and that she was preventing Jim from seeing his family.

Martha's manipulative hooks were embedded very deeply in Sally. The guilt and conflict with Jim were causing considerable stress and strain in the new marriage. When Sally announced that she was pregnant, Martha raised her control maneuvers to a new level. No matter what Sally and Jim said they wanted to do, Martha seemed able to override their wishes and to manipulate Sally into compliance with her demands, often at Jim's and/or Sally's expense.

This is when an agitated Jim and a very pregnant Sally walked into my office.

Act Three: Location, Location, Location

Five minutes after Francine started telling me why she had come to see me, I already knew the punch line. Her story—rather, her *type* of story—was very familiar to me.

Francine was an attractive 26-year-old, working as a commercial real estate broker at a prestigious firm. She had been at the firm about 2 years when Arnie, a seasoned 38-year-old senior broker, approached her and asked her out to lunch. Arnie was one of the top performers in the firm, and she was flattered that he even knew her name. And, she was thrilled to find out that Arnie had what appeared to be a lucrative business proposition for her.

It is common in brokerage offices for two brokers to get together and form a partnership. It is also common for a more seasoned broker to take a young protégé under his or her wing and teach him or her the ropes. But Francine was surprised that the top broker in the office asked her to come under his guidance.

Arnie's proposal was along these lines: He explained that his wife was pregnant with their second child. He had worked long hours and weekends to build his career soon after he and his wife married. While he was building financial security, he had missed out on much of his son's growing up. He regretted missing so many soccer and little league games, musical recitals, and school plays.

But now that he was going to have a second child, he wanted to cut back on his grueling work schedule to spend more time with his wife and family. In fact, he no longer wanted to work *any* weekends or late evenings if he could possibly avoid it. His partnership proposal with Francine was simple and—by the way—fairly common. After a probationary period of about 6 months, they would formalize the relationship in writing. He would then cut her in on all his deals in exchange for her doing the brunt of the legwork, the research, the late hours, and the weekend work. She would learn a lot and eventually—Arnie never specified when exactly—get very rich.

Francine jumped at the chance, and they shook hands. In truth, aside from being deliriously happy about what was said at the meeting, she also was delighted to realize that this was a firm that allowed an employee to have a successful career and a family. While she was still single, she hoped one day to have a husband and family. She was reassured to know that she worked for a company that would support her striving to "have it all."

Francine never worked as hard as she did for the next 6 months. Arnie was a natural business getter, and he kept her hopping. She was knee-deep involved in every deal and often was in the office past midnight and on virtually every week-end. She willingly gave up having any kind of social life for a while. Arnie left work early and never came in on week-ends. "That's okay," she told herself. "This is what I signed up for."

After 6 months, she anxiously waited for Arnie to for-mally end her probationary period and allow her to reap some of the financial benefits that had been promised her. But Arnie said nothing.

She waited about 2 weeks and tentatively broached the subject with him, telling herself that he was so busy that he probably had forgotten. However, when she started to raise the subject, he exploded in a rage and threatened to cancel the whole arrangement.

Francine was stunned and retreated to her cubicle like a wounded kitten.

The next day he apologized for his outburst but did not raise the subject about when her probationary period would end. She decided to wait another week to bring the subject up again, unless he did first. But he did not.

From then on, whenever she did talk to Arnie about when she would begin to see some financial rewards, he would lec-ture her about trust and threaten to pull out of their arrange-ment if she did not have faith in him. Finally, Francine convinced herself to trust Arnie, reasoning or rationalizing that this might be his way of testing her loyalty. She vowed to herself not to broach the subject again. And she didn't, as another 3 months went by.

Late one Saturday afternoon as she was preparing to leave the office, the phone rang on Arnie's desk. Francine answered it, as she was accustomed to doing, and found herself talking to Arnie's wife, Phyllis. Phyllis asked if she could speak with

Arnie. Naturally, Francine said he was not there. Then Phyllis asked when he had left. And Francine caught herself as she was about to say the truth—which was that Arnie had not been there all day. He *never* worked on weekends.

Sensing a problem and not wanting to get Arnie in trouble, Francine lied and said that she had just arrived and did not know when Arnie left. The conversation ended cordially, and Francine put it out of her mind.

However, the same thing happened the following Saturday. Arnie's wife called looking for him or asking what time he had left the office. Again, Francine covered for Arnie, but this time—being unable to resist her own curiosity—she managed to discern that Phyllis believed that Arnie had been coming to work with Francine every Saturday for at least 6 months.

Francine was confused. The following Monday she was determined to speak to Arnie, but when she tried to bring up the subject of Phyllis's call and the fact that she thought he was in the office every Saturday while she, Francine, thought he was at home with his wife and family, Arnie exploded in a rage.

Badly shaken and not knowing what to do, Francine turned to one of the other young female associate brokers in the office who was a casual friend of hers. Francine was in for another shock. Her friend was surprised that Francine did not know that Arnie was having an affair with a young woman trainee in the office. Everyone—except Francine—apparently knew that Arnie was quite the womanizer and had been sexually involved with several female brokers as well as clients.

Francine made some other discrete inquiries among her office coworkers. Arnie's extramarital activities were common knowledge. Arnie, it appeared, had been cheating on his wife since the day he was married. In fact, most of the people she spoke with thought that Francine was romantically involved with Arnie because of their "cozy relationship."

Francine protested and tried to explain it was "all business." Some of her coworkers laughingly replied, "Oh, sure; right."

That bastard! Francine thought. He's been using me to do his work and promising that my big payday is just around the corner. He tells me he wants to spend time with his wife and kids on the weekends, so I do all the heavy work. Then I find out he's been cheating on his wife and hasn't been home on a weekend in 6 months. And he lectures me about trust and loyalty!

Arnie had manipulated her for nearly 9 months, and she had nothing to show for it except exhaustion, stress, no social life, a damaged reputation, and egg on her face.

This is when she came to see me.

Act Four: Terrible Teens

What is worse than being the new girl in tenth grade?

Cara's father was a successful film director in New York who took a job in Hollywood with one of the major studios. He and his wife and 15-year-old daughter moved to California late in the summer, just in time for Cara to enter tenth grade at a local school.

Back East, Cara had been considered "popular." Her mother always made sure that she had the latest "in" clothes and gave cool parties. It was not easy for Cara to give up her friends and move to a new city, but she was determined to make the best of it.

Cara's mother tried to reassure her that she would soon be friends with the "cool" kids at the new school. In fact, though,

Cara's mother had a lot of anxiety about Cara's adjustment. Her mother had grown up as an "army brat"—an officer's daughter—who had a tough time adapting to new schools and new kids every few years with her father's new postings.

"Just be yourself," her mother advised, trying to cover her own worries. "The popular crowd will welcome you with open arms. You'll see."

But things did not go as planned. There definitely was a "cool" crowd at her new school, but they could not be bothered with Cara. She was not one of them, and her clothes were all wrong. Cara actually overheard two girls making fun of her fashion style. She was mortified.

However, she also was determined to succeed. She studied what the girls wore and immediately saw that there was a difference between East Coast cool and West Coast cool. She preferred her own style but was willing to change if it would get her in with the coveted crowd.

She went home after that first day in tears. She told her mother that she hated her clothes and needed new things to fit in with everyone else. Not wanting her daughter to be left out, her mother took Cara to the mall that night. They did a major shopping run to last them through the rest of the week. That weekend Cara threw out all her "old" clothes, and mother and daughter hit the stores again.

On the following Monday, desperate to be included, Cara asked if she could join the "popular" crowd at lunch. They reluctantly moved over and let her hang off the end of the bench where they were eating lunch. One of the girls complimented her outfit, which made Cara feel better. It was an icebreaker. Another asked what her parents did, and Cara bragged about her father's fame. She also let it be known that her family had money. When she opened her wallet once to pay for a soft drink, they could see wads of money stuffed inside. With newfound interest, the girls began talking about where to get clothes and shoes and makeup. By the end of lunch, Cara thought she was making some real social headway.

However, these "popular" girls did not let just anyone into their inner sanctum. And it was obvious to them that Cara would do anything to be popular. So they decided to let her "buy" her way in.

When they would go for sodas or ice cream after school, they let Cara treat them. If they went out for pizza, Cara got stuck with the check. Although she was sometimes included in after-school shopping or trips to restaurants, she still had not been invited to parties with the "cool" boys. When Cara mustered her nerve to ask about the parties, a few of the girls suggested that she might be included soon.

Meanwhile, Cara's mom—who was my patient—was not oblivious to all that was going on. Because of her own anxieties and bad experiences as a teenager, Cara's mother was an easy touch. Cara could manipulate her mom into giving her more and more money so that she could accommodate her friends. When her so-called friends did not invite her to their Saturday night parties, her mother did not have the heart to tell her daughter that she was just being used. However, she did strongly encourage Cara to make friends with lots of different girls. Sadly, as far as Cara was concerned, it was too late for that. There were some girls who had tried to befriend her, but since they were not part of the in crowd, Cara treated them badly and rebuffed their invitations to join them for lunch or sodas after school. In her mind, she had definitely burned that bridge.

Then a couple of the popular girls approached Cara with a proposition: "Show us you know how to throw a super cool party," they said, "and you can join our crowd." The girls even had a party in mind: a full day at a local spa where they would all be pampered and massaged, polished, and primped.

Cara knew that she could convince her father to pay for the spa party.

When her father got home, Cara laid on the guilt trip, big time. She told her father that it was his idea to move here and that it was his fault she was having a tough time making new friends. She even cried. She told him about the party idea, and he readily agreed, if only to stop his guilt and his daughter's tears.

The next day Cara announced that the party was on for Saturday in 2 weeks. The girls responded by providing her with the "approved" guest list of 15 girls. When Cara told her mother about the party and the list of 15, her mom calculated the cost at more than $250 per girl. Her mom demanded that the guest list be limited to 7 girls, or else the party would have to be canceled.

When Cara's mom dropped this bomb, Cara went nuclear. She exploded in hysterics. Through her tears and her anguish, Cara explained that she could not possibly cancel the party after she had announced it was on. She would be humiliated and never have any friends. If she "uninvited" any of the people on the list now, she would be a social reject forever.

Reluctantly, her mother capitulated after 3 hours of Cara's unrelenting emotional blast.

The party seemed to be a huge hit. All the girls said they had a great time. Cara went to sleep that night with a smile on her face for the first time since she had moved out west.

The smile lasted until Monday morning. When she showed up at school, Cara expected to be welcomed as one of the in crowd. But the in crowd was very fickle. Now that they had gotten what they wanted from Cara, they had no further use for her. She was suddenly cast aside, subjected to a cold shoulder from all her party guests.

They had manipulated her mercilessly, knowing that as long as they kept holding out the promise of acceptance, they could bend her anyway they wanted. It was their pattern. They had done this many times before with other wanna-bes.

Of course, along the way, Cara did her share of manipulating her parents—especially her insecure mother—to indulge her expensive whims so that she could buy her popularity.

Cara's mother felt responsible for her daughter's pain. That Monday afternoon, Cara's mother brought her distraught daughter for a session of joint family therapy.

Act Five: Double Squeeze

Valerie's clock is ticking, and this is making her very nervous. Valerie is 37 years old and never married. She and Jay dated for 3 years before they moved in together 2 years ago. He was married once but has no children.

From the beginning of their relationship, Valerie was clear and outspoken about her desire both to marry and to have children. On his part, Jay said he loved kids and would love to be a dad as long as he was with the right woman and certain that his second marriage would be successful. The son of divorced parents, Jay said that he never wanted his own kids to experience that kind of pain.

Jay's first marriage ended in a very acrimonious divorce, and it cost him a lot of money and heartache. It also left him badly scarred and very cautious about making another commitment and risking another failure.

Valerie asserted that she was the "right woman" for Jay. By the time Valerie moved in with Jay, she felt that there was definitely the hint of matrimony in the air, but no promise. However, as soon as she unpacked her bags, that hint seemed to vanish.

Shortly after they moved in together, Valerie raised the subject of marriage. Jay explained that that while he loved Valerie, he was going to be very sure before making another "final" commitment because of his bad experience last time. He asked her, "Believe in me. Give me time. I just need to be sure. Now, let's change the subject." And he refused to discuss the topic further.

Over time, Jay grew increasingly irritable when Valerie even alluded to marriage.

At the end of their first year of living together, Valerie expected a ring. She got flowers instead. Valerie could not hide her disappointment. Tearfully, she insisted that they talk about their future.

Jay angrily refused to talk. They argued heatedly for several minutes over Jay's unwillingness to even listen to Valerie's needs and concerns. Then Jay stood up and yelled, "Look what's happening—we're fighting! I knew this sort of thing would happen. This is just what I want to avoid in a marriage. My first marriage was just like this, too—fighting all the time. Until I know we can get along better, there sure isn't going to be any wedding!" And he stormed out of the house.

Valerie composed herself. She loved Jay and was afraid that he would leave her if she pushed the issue too hard. She told herself to give him a little more time, and she admonished herself to be more patient. Jay returned home a few hours later. Valerie apologized for upsetting him and asked his forgiveness. Jay remained aloof and withholding for a few days before he finally thawed, and their normally happy companionship resumed.

After that, if Valerie did bring up the subject of marriage or kids even tangentially, she could sense Jay's jaw tightening. She knew that there would be another angry outburst and fight if she did not immediately back down and change the subject. The truth was that Jay's anger scared her. The irony was that Valerie was not a fighter. She loathed conflict and confrontation and went to great lengths to avoid them.

However, the truth also was that she was not getting any younger, her biological clock was ticking louder and louder, and she still was not engaged. As her frustration mounted, so did her own anger, which she tried hard to suppress.

This was a classic double squeeze. Jay had manipulated her into a position where if she said nothing, she could avoid his anger—but not be married. If she was honest about her feelings, they would certainly argue, and he would then say, "Aha! This is just what I'm afraid of if we get married." Her worst fear was that Jay would tire of the conflict and simply leave her altogether.

Valerie was caught on the horns of manipulation with her fondest dreams of marriage and kids hanging in limbo. This is when she came to see me.

Now that you have had a look at how manipulation works in five real-life examples, let's turn to your own life experience. In Chapter 3 you will have a chance to assess how vulnerable you may be to the tactics of manipulation.

3

Are You Vulnerable to Manipulation?

ANYONE AND EVERYONE is potentially vulnerable to the control of a skilled manipulator—especially one who keeps his or her motives, intentions, and methods carefully disguised or concealed. However, while virtually anyone *can* be manipulated depending on the particular circumstances, some people are walking targets: They seem to be marked for manipulation.

Such people display certain personality traits, behaviors, and ways of thinking that render them extremely vulnerable to manipulative control. As you will learn in Chapter 4, these tendencies form the "buttons" that manipulators push in order to bring such people into their web of coercive influence.

Are you an easy mark for manipulators? Take the quiz below and find out.

Are You a Soft Target for Manipulators?

Read each statement below. If the statement is true or mostly true for you, circle T; if it is false or mostly false, circle F. Be sure to circle either T or F for every item. No fence-sitting.

1. I should always try to please other people   T   F
   and make them happy.
2. I have always needed the approval of other   T   F
   people.
3. Other people should be kind and caring to   T   F
   me in return because of how well I treat them.
4. I often feel that I do not have a clear sense   T   F
   of my own identity.
5. Other people should never reject or criticize   T   F
   me because I always try my best to live up
   to their expectations, needs, and desires.
6. It is very difficult for me to turn down a   T   F
   request from a friend, family member, or
   someone at work.
7. Often, being nice prevents me from   T   F
   expressing negative feelings toward others.
8. I believe that nothing good can come from   T   F
   conflict.
9. I believe that most of the things that happen   T   F
   to me are more in the control of other
   people than within my own control.
10. I am always deeply concerned about what   T   F
    others think of me in nearly every area of
    my life.
11. I should always try to do what others want,   T   F
    expect, or need from me.
12. I would feel very guilty if I did not make the   T   F
    needs of others more important than my own.
13. I tend to rely more on the opinions and   T   F
    judgments of others than I do on my own
    opinions and judgments.
14. My sense of self-worth and value comes   T   F
    from how much I do for others.

15. I believe that people like me because of all the things I do for them. T F

16. I very seldom say no to anyone who needs my help or wants me to do a favor. T F

17. I have a great deal of trouble making decisions on my own. T F

18. I would have difficulty describing who I really am or what I think, feel, or believe independent of how other people see me. T F

19. I am easily intimidated by another person's display of anger or hostility. T F

20. Other people should never be angry with me because I would go to any length to avoid conflict, anger, or confrontation with them. T F

21. It is extremely important to me to be liked by nearly everyone in my life. T F

22. I feel that I need to earn other people's love or approval by doing things to make them happy. T F

23. I often say yes when I would like to say no to requests from others. T F

24. I would go to almost any length to avoid a confrontation. T F

25. I believe that other people would question my value as a person if I did not do things for them. T F

26. I believe that luck, opportunity, and the goodwill of others have much more to do with what happens to me than anything that I do by myself. T F

27. I should always try to put other people first, before me. T F

28. I think it is my responsibility to calm down   T   F
    people around me if they become agitated,
    angry or aggressive.
29. I often feel confused by all the feedback I   T   F
    get from others about how to run my life.
30. I want everyone to think of me as a nice person.   T   F
31. I believe that I am usually to blame if   T   F
    someone gets angry with me.
32. I almost never disagree with or challenge   T   F
    another's opinion for fear that I might
    provoke an angry conflict or confrontation.
33. If I stopped putting others' needs ahead of   T   F
    my own, I would become a selfish person
    and people would not like me.
34. I believe that I should always be nice even   T   F
    if it means allowing others to take advantage
    of my good nature.
35. I feel that my value is almost entirely   T   F
    derived from the things I do for others and
    from what others think of me.
36. I rely a lot on what other people think of   T   F
    me to form my self-concept and self-esteem.
37. I generally have to ask lots of people for their   T   F
    input about nearly every decision I make.
38. I do not think that there is really very much   T   F
    I can do to prevent or minimize negative
    things from happening to me.
39. I seem to need everyone's approval before I   T   F
    make an important decision.
40. I believe that it is best just to smile and   T   F
    cover up angry feelings than to express
    them and risk getting into a fight or conflict.

How to Score and Interpret Your Answers

Give yourself a score of 1 for every T you circled. Give yourself a score of 0 for every F you circled.

If your score is between 31 and 40, you are extremely vulnerable to manipulation. It is quite likely that several other people have been pulling your strings for most of your life. At this point, you are virtually a guaranteed "soft target" for a manipulator.

If your score is between 21 and 30, you are very vulnerable to manipulation. You have likely experienced several manipulative relationships in your life and remain quite vulnerable to further manipulation in the future.

If your score is between 11 and 20, you are somewhat susceptible to manipulation. Under the right circumstances, a manipulator could well gain control over you.

If your score is between 1 and 10, you are only slightly vulnerable to manipulation. However, you are not entirely invulnerable; nobody is.

If you scored a 0, you are not an easy target for a manipulator. However, you would be unwise to believe that you are completely invulnerable to manipulation. Remember, *anybody* can fall prey to a skilled manipulator under the right circumstances. It is possible that those circumstances have yet to visit you.

Review the statements that you marked true. Think about how each statement might be used by a manipulative person out to gain control over you. In fact, each of the statements represents part of a belief system that forms the underpinning for your behavior, moods, and personality traits. These beliefs are the buttons that manipulators push because they detect them as your vulnerability points. As you will soon understand, the buttons represent flawed ways of thinking that set you up as an easy mark for a manipulator.

In Chapter 4 you will learn more about how and why these ways of thinking make you so vulnerable to manipulation. Later, in Chapter 13, you will get a healthy dose of cognitive therapy designed to correct your flawed thinking and to make you a far harder and more resilient target for manipulation.

4

Your Buttons
Are Showing

IN THIS CHAPTER we will begin to examine
more closely the personality traits and tendencies that make you a mark for manipulators.
My purpose here is to help you to become more aware of the
"buttons" of vulnerability that you unwittingly expose to
other people and that set you up as a mark for manipulation.
Later in this book we will turn to what you can do to make
yourself a hardened target for manipulators, thereby making
you less vulnerable to coercive control.

It is not my purpose here to explain how and why you
developed these areas of vulnerability. In a real sense, "Why"
is a luxury question. It may be interesting to discover why you
became a marked target, but it is far more important to change
your thinking and behaviors and to reduce your vulnerability.
So *why* you developed areas of manipulative vulnerability is
far less important to the goals of this book than developing
your awareness of them and ultimately developing ways to
protect yourself from manipulation.

It is important to reiterate that *anyone* and *everyone* is
potentially vulnerable to the control of a skilled manipulator—

especially one who keeps his or her motives, intentions, and methods carefully disguised and concealed, often even to himself or herself. If you are a victim, you are not alone. As you will soon learn, however, certain people are very easy or soft targets for a manipulator's purposes. You know your vulnerability score from Chapter 3. Since you may well be one of those who are marked for manipulation, let's take a look at how potential manipulators spot you.

What Are Your Buttons?

What buttons do manipulators push to pressure you? People who are marked for manipulation display some or all of seven areas of vulnerability in their personalities. These characteristic ways of thinking, feeling, and behaving with other people make them vulnerable and receptive to the tactics of manipulators.

Think of these seven areas as your buttons that manipulators push. Whether you realize it or not, your buttons are showing. Manipulative people, through lots of experience controlling others to serve their own needs and purposes, have a sixth sense for spotting their marks. They do so by picking up the clues to your personality, which they can exploit. Often they are able to do this simply because you tip your hand and freely expose your buttons. When you do this, it is called a *tell*.

It is highly likely that you may find yourself vulnerable in multiple areas—with all or nearly all your buttons resonating with my descriptions. This is to be expected because the buttons are psychologically interconnected areas.

The first step toward the safe zone—away from manipulative relationships—depends on your ability to identify, recognize, and understand these buttons or areas of vulnerability in yourself. Chances are that you probably have already identified some or all of these areas as sources of stress or problems in your life; however, you may not fully understand how much of a role they play in setting you up for repetitive experiences as the victim of manipulation.

Button No. 1: You Have the Disease to Please— People-Pleasing Habits and Mind-Sets

Those who have the "disease to please" have people-pleasing habits and mind-sets, and this is not good. People-pleasing is an odd problem. At first glance, it may not even seem like a problem at all. In fact, the label *people-pleaser* may feel more like a compliment or a flattering self-description that you proudly wear as a badge of honor. Isn't it all right to be a people-pleaser? Shouldn't this, by definition, be a good thing?

The truth is that people-pleasing is a sweet-sounding name for a pattern of thinking, feeling, and acting that can become a serious and far-reaching psychological problem. The "disease to please," or the people-pleasing syndrome, is a compulsive—even addictive—pattern. As a people-pleaser, you feel controlled by your need to please others and virtually addicted to their approval. At the same time, you feel out of control over the pressures and demands on your life that these needs have created.

If you have the "disease to please," your need to please others is not limited to just saying yes a little too often or to occasionally going overboard in doing nice things for other people. Instead, if you are a people-pleaser, your emotional tuning dials are jammed on the frequency of what you believe other people want or expect of you. Just the perception that another might need your help is enough to send your people-pleasing response system into overdrive.

The problem is that when you have the "disease to please," your self-esteem is all tied up with how much you do for others and how successful you are at pleasing them. You may think that by fulfilling the needs of others, you have the magic formula for gaining love and self-worth and for protecting yourself from abandonment and rejection. However, the reality is that the formula is badly flawed. It does not work. Moreover, people-pleasing causes you harm because you take care of everyone else's needs *at the expense of your own.*

People-pleasers pay far too high a price for being *nice.* If you are a bona fide people-pleaser, you will know how central the concept of *nice* is to your identity. People-pleasers become deeply attached to seeing themselves—and to being certain that others see them—as *nice* people. Their very identity hinges on *niceness.*

The price of nice, however, is that other people can and will manipulate and exploit your willingness to please them. Your niceness may even blind you to the fact that you are being manipulated and exploited. After all, it wouldn't be *nice* to question the motives of the very people you are breaking your neck to please, would it?

To make matters worse, even if you do suspect that you are being manipulated, you are too nice to confront, criticize, or have the kind of direct, frank, and candid conversation that is necessary to stop a manipulator and to protect your own self-interest.

The thinking of people-pleasers is contaminated and distorted by toxic and self-sabotaging *shoulds.* Complying with these *shoulds* is what causes the high levels of stress that result from people-pleasing. The *shoulds* also perpetuate your vulnerability to manipulation by others.

The mind-sets of people-pleasing can be boiled down to two credos, the first of which I call "The 10 Commandments of People-Pleasing":

1. I should always do what others want, expect, or need from me.
2. I should take care of everyone around me whether they ask for my help or not.
3. I should always listen to everyone's problems and try my best to solve them, whether I am asked to or not.
4. I should always be nice and never hurt anyone's feelings.
5. I should always put other people first, before me.
6. I should never say no to anyone who need or requests something of me.
7. I should never disappoint anyone or let others down in any way.
8. I should always be happy and upbeat and never show any negative feelings to others.
9. I should always try to please other people and make them happy.
10. I should try never to burden others with my own needs or problems.

The second credo of people-pleasing I call "The Seven Deadly Shoulds" for others' behavior:

1. Other people should appreciate and love me because of all the things I do for them.
2. Other people should always like and approve of me because of how hard I work to please them.

3. Other people should never reject or criticize me because I always try to live up to their desires and expectations.
4. Other people should be kind and caring to me in return because of how well I treat them.
5. Other people should never hurt me or treat me unfairly because I am so nice to them.
6. Other people should never leave or abandon me because of how much I make them need me.
7. Other people should never be angry with me because I would go to any length to avoid conflict, anger, or confrontation with them.

The *shoulds* of people-pleasing set you up for manipulation by guilt and obligation. Having an *excessive* sense of responsibility for the welfare and happiness of others is the lever that manipulators will use when they invoke guilt or obligation to control your behavior. Even worse, just the anticipation of feeling guilty—and the need to avoid feeling guilty—is what you use to manipulate yourself into doing things that you may not want to do.

People-pleasers frequently justify and explain their compliance or collusion with manipulators by stating that they cannot stand to feel guilty, so they give in to whatever the demand—often even to just the anticipation of the demand.

People-pleasing habits and mind-sets are an obvious tell or a dead give-away. If you have the "disease to please," manipulators can spot you coming a mile away.

Button No. 2: You Are Addicted to Earning the Approval and Acceptance of Others

When you are "hooked," you feel that you *must* earn the approval and acceptance of others—*all* others. Moreover, you need to avoid criticism, rejection, and abandonment at almost any price.

At the core of your niceness is a dread fear of rejection and abandonment. If you are a people-pleaser, you believe that by being nice and always doing things for others—even at your own expense—you will avoid the feelings that you so dread.

There is nothing wrong or unhealthy about valuing the approval of others, especially those you love and respect. Wanting to be liked by others is a perfectly natural human desire. However, if your desire to be liked and approved of by others becomes *mandatory*—when it feels essential to your emotional survival, and the consequences of disapproval, rejection, or criticism seem catastrophic—you have crossed over into dangerous psychological territory. You will find yourself in manipulation territory and under the thumb of manipulators' coercive control.

When the approval of others becomes more than desirable—when it becomes *imperative*—you have become a mark for manipulation. If you are an approval addict, your behavior is as easy to control as that of any other junkie. All a manipulator need do is a simple two-step process: Give you what you crave, and then threaten to take it away.

Every drug dealer in the world plays this game. And since you are an approval addict, the social world poses an ongoing threat of loss.

First, the manipulator will let you earn his or her approval and acceptance. Keep in mind, however, that like any addict, you will consume whatever approval, acceptance, and displays of positive regard that you receive. There is no storage or banking of approval in your psychological economy. However much approval and liking you may gain today, it simply will not last; you will feel the craving for approval again tomorrow. And however much approval you have been given today, you will face your dreaded fear of losing that approval and acceptance tomorrow. It is a vicious cycle—and one that manipulators play adroitly.

Therefore, step 2 is abundantly clear: Once you are hooked on the approval and acceptance of the manipulator, all he or she needs to do is merely threaten to withdraw them. Actually, since you are an approval addict, the threat of withdrawal can even remain implicit. In other words, no one needs to verbalize or overtly threaten to reject you or to take away his or her approval or acceptance of you. The threat exists in the very air you breathe.

Paradoxically, the more you identify with being nice and pleasing others to guarantee and ensure their approval and acceptance of you, the more insecure you will become. The more you identify with being nice, instead of being *real*, the more you will find yourself plagued by nagging doubts and insecurities and lingering fears.

If your approval addiction is deeply entrenched, the button that will show most clearly to manipulators is your willingness to do nearly anything to avoid disapproval, rejection, and worst of all, abandonment.

In love relationships or romantic entanglements that become manipulative, fear of abandonment is the ultimate lever of control.

Button No. 3: You Have "Emotophobia"—Fear of Negative Emotions

Cognitive therapist David Burns coined the term "emotophobia" to refer to an excessive or irrational fear of negative feelings. Specifically, these fears encompass anger, aggression, or hostility and the conflict and confrontation that arouse them. If this is your hot button, you will go to almost any lengths to *avoid* anger, conflict, and confrontation.

The manipulator's task is relatively easy if your fear of conflict, confrontation, and anger button is showing. A manipulator can readily control your behavior through tactics of intimidation—easily achieved by merely raising his or her voice and/or hinting that anger may be on the verge of breaking through. When this button is showing, a manipulator needs only to make you sense that anger or conflict may erupt. You are likely to comply with the manipulation just to avoid even the mere possibility that anger or conflict may emerge.

Soon you may even do the manipulator's job for him: You may conjure up in your mind a scenario that involves the manipulator's anger, and you take action to avoid it even though no anger has yet occurred. The manipulator may not even be around. However, your "emotophobia" is so strong that you can play out the manipulator's reaction in your mind and allow yourself to be manipulated as a result.

The really dangerous aspect about fearing negative emotions is that the longer you avoid dealing with them, the more threatening and uncontrollable they feel. And the more you *avoid* dealing with negative emotions, the less able you become to deal with them effectively and appropriately.

Ironically, while you may not be fully aware of this connection, the more you allow manipulators to control your behavior, the angrier *you* are likely to become.

Is it possible—even desirable—to avoid all anger, conflict, or confrontation? The fact of the matter is that negative emotions are built into the hardwiring of human beings. What this means is that all of us are programmed biologically to feel anger and to respond defensively when others seek to harm us or hurt those for whom we love or care. It is neither possible nor desirable to be entirely rid of negative feelings.

Anger is not necessarily bad or unhealthy. Repressing or chronically suppressing anger by going to great lengths to camouflage, disguise, ignore, or otherwise avoid it is unhealthy. How many times have you found yourself outwardly denying your anger and resentment toward another person—especially when that person is manipulating and controlling you—while on the inside you feel anxious, panicked, and depressed?

Depression, by one psychological definition, is the result of anger that you turn against yourself. Symptoms of anxiety, sleeplessness, and irritability abound in relationships where there is inadequate communication and an inability to confront problems directly in order to reach greater understanding and resolution.

Conflict can and should be handled constructively; when it is, relationships benefit. Conflict avoidance is *not* the hallmark of a good relationship. On the contrary, it is a symptom of serious problems and of poor communication.

Button No. 4: Lack of Assertiveness and an Inability to Say No

If you are a people-pleaser who seeks everyone's approval (buttons 1 and 2), you are likely to fall into the category of a person who has a great deal of trouble saying no. While the word *nice* may be the best singular description of people-pleasers' personalities, the word *no* generally does not appear in their vocabularies. If you are a people-pleaser, it is a safe bet that you have difficulty saying no to just about any request, expressed need, desire, invitation, or demand—implicit or explicit—from nearly anyone.

Saying no probably makes you feel guilty or selfish because you equate it with disappointing and letting others down. After years of saying yes, you have taught others to expect you to comply. Now you may feel that saying yes is simply your only option.

Obviously, your inability to set limits and boundaries and to say no to some of the people some of the time makes you an obvious mark for manipulation. If you cannot say no, how difficult is it for just about anyone to get you to do what he or she wants? Lack of assertiveness makes you putty in the hands of a skilled manipulator.

Just the idea or possibility of saying no may be enough to make you feel uncomfortably tense and anxious. And each time you give into your fears and say yes, the short-term anxiety reduction merely strengthens your yes-saying habits. However, the longer-term consequences of your knee-jerk compliance are costly for you and highly advantageous to the manipulators in your life.

If you are like most people-pleasers, your aversion to saying no is probably grounded in the negative angry responses that you anticipate your denial might elicit. In this sense, the lack of assertiveness button is closely connected to the fear of negative emotions and the strong need to avoid conflict and confrontation.

If you fear that saying no might set off another person's anger or engender a conflict between you, and if you are inclined to go out of your way to avoid conflict and confrontation, then your yes-saying habits will become more deeply ingrained and harder to change each time you comply. And those who manipulate you are continually rewarded for their actions by your willing compliance.

Saying no may make you feel guilty, anxious, and uncomfortable because the years of suppressing your urge to say no have been generating continuous frustration. Given the chance to vent, that frustration could erupt into raging anger. It is not surprising, then, that the mere prospect of lifting the ban on saying no floods you with anxiety. Your fear has far more to do with your long-suppressed resentment and with the intensely angry and offensive way that you might finally say no—or rather scream "NO!"—than with the mere use of the word itself.

However, as you may already have learned, when you always say yes (especially when you really want to say no), eventually you will find yourself joylessly going through the motions of living—yielding control over your precious time and resources to the will of whoever asks for it. In effect, your continuous yes saying will enslave you to others who seek to control and manipulate you.

Your avoidance of saying no also may be linked to the self-esteem you think you earn by doing things for others. In this sense, by saying no to a request, you also will be denying yourself an opportunity to add one more count to the sum of tasks and favors you accomplish on behalf of others. If you are a hard-core people-pleaser, your self-worth depends on the things you do for other people, and your reluctance to turn down a chance to add another point to your tally of accomplishments is easily understandable.

However, the dilemma you face if you are a constant people-pleaser who cannot be assertive and say no some of the time to some of the people in your life is that the time will come when your energy *will* run out, despite your best intentions and your impressive ability to meet almost everyone's needs at least so far. In the meanwhile, you will cede more and more control over yourself to those who manipulate you by asking or just expecting you to do what they ask or require each and every time they need you.

Learning to say no is imperative to becoming less vulnerable to manipulation.

Button No. 5: The Vanishing Self

People with "vanishing selves" have only a blurry sense of their own identity, where they begin and end, whose needs they feel and fill, and what values are central to their core. Does this describe you?

This button is both a cause and a consequence of being the victim of ongoing manipulation. The longer you allow yourself to be the pawn in other people's games, the less clear your own identity will seem to you and to others who perceive you.

You will know if this button applies to you if you can agree with the statement that you do not know who you really are and what you really stand for outside of the things you do for other people. Some people with a diminished sense of self describe the experience as feeling *invisible*—unseen and unrecognized by others as having a set of needs and characteristics that stand independently of others. You even may experience dreams or waking sensations of shrinking or literally diminishing in size.

The causes of a fuzzy identity and a blurry sense of self are generally rooted in childhood experiences that interfered with a healthy development of self. This may be due to negative parental feedback—or negative input from other important people in the child's life—in which that child hears repeatedly and eventually "learns" that his or her opinion does not matter or count, that he or she is not smart or capable, or that he or she is expected to always bend to the will of more powerful or authoritative others.

When your identity is fuzzy and out of focus, you will feel alienated from yourself and from others. When you do not clearly present yourself to others and define your boundaries by setting appropriate limits, saying no, and standing up for your own rights, others will tend to project their notions of who you are—or, more accurately, of who they need you to be—onto your identity.

Psychologists use a classic test to analyze personality. It is called the *Rorschach,* and it is a series of cards, each of which contains an inkblot—an ambiguous image that the individual being tested is requested to "see" as a picture. The theory is that the individual will project onto the ambiguous inkblot what he or she *needs* to see.

When you present yourself in the world with an ambiguous sense of identity, you invite others to shape you according to their needs and desires. This is what I call the *Rorschach phenomenon.*

People who have blurry identities and vanishing senses of self are fodder for the mill of manipulators. Over time, the participation in manipulative relationships merely weakens and erodes the victim's identity further and further.

Without a strong, clear sense of your own identity, you are highly vulnerable and a near-certain mark for manipulation.

Button No. 6: Low Self-Reliance

Low self-reliance means that you distrust your own judgment and reactions, resulting in an impairment of your self-direction. This button is closely related to button 5.

If your sense of self is blurry and unclear, your ability to rely on your own judgment will be impaired. If you cannot depend on yourself and your own judgment and values to guide you in your decision making—especially when it pertains to relationships in which others seek to manipulate you—you will necessarily be more prone to rely on the judgments and direction of others.

Being a self-directed person is the opposite of being a mark for manipulators. If you lack the ability to consult yourself or to rely on the judgments or values that you hold, your dependence on others will increase, and your vulnerability to being controlled by what others want you to do for them—to serve their purposes and advance their gains—will be almost ensured.

People who have low self-esteem are less likely to be self-reliant than those with high self-esteem, and not surprisingly, those who rely on themselves more often in making determinations in their relationships with other people will raise their self-esteem by doing so. In short, if you do not think much of yourself—and particularly if you cannot even see yourself very clearly (button 5)—you will not be inclined to exercise independence, autonomy, and self-reliance in your actions with others.

Instead, your dependence on others' judgments, opinions, and decision making will be far greater than your reliance on your own, thereby ushering the way in for manipulators of all types.

People with low self-reliance will recognize the tendency in themselves to ask other people—almost everyone they know—for their input and advice regarding an impending decision or problem or for input about a purchase, a hairstyle, a menu for entertaining, a business practice—or just about anything else that requires them to take a position. Often, asking too many other people for advice merely confuses the issue further, and lacking confidence in their own ability to sort through and assimilate the various sources of advice they have so ardently sought, such people now feel the need to ask others to help them process what everyone else has said. Making any kind of decision makes them feel anxious and unsure.

Improving your decision-making ability and particularly your skills at resolving postdecisional regret—also known as *buyer's remorse*—will go a long way toward increasing self-reliance. Without the ability to rely on your own judgments and to make your own decisions by acting as a reliable counselor to yourself, you will continue to be a prime mark for manipulation.

Button No. 7: External Locus of Control

Locus of control (LOC) is a psychological phrase that refers to how and where you attribute the cause of the things that happen, or fail to happen, to you. People that have an *external* LOC have the general view that the things that happen to them in life are more under the control of others and of factors outside of themselves than under their own control. In contrast, people who have an *internal* LOC believe that the primary source of control over what happens to them in life lies within themselves.

LOC reflects your experiences in life and the ways you have been taught to understand and look at the world. Having an internal LOC does not mean that you think you are in control of *everything,* nor does it mean that you lack faith in a higher power or that you do not recognize the realistic limits of what you can control and what you cannot. Believing that you are in control of the weather, for example, is not a reflection of a healthy internal LOC but rather a delusional perception that simply is not in line with reality.

On the other hand, believing that the relative success of your career is largely up to you and believing that the grades you get in school are under the control of your ability and effort are examples of an appropriate and healthy internal LOC.

Research shows that people who have an internal LOC have higher self-esteem than those with an external LOC. Consequently, people with an internal LOC are less at risk for falling prey to a manipulator.

Another term that psychologists use to invoke this dimension of personality is a variable called *personal efficacy*. People who have a high degree of personal efficacy have the sense that they have mastery over their environments—or the ability to make the things that they want to happen come to pass. Those with a low degree of personal efficacy do not have a sense of mastery. They do not feel like effective players in making things happen in their lives and, consequently, do not exert the same degree of directed, self-generated effort as those with both an internal LOC and high personal efficacy.

It stands to reason that if you believe that other people have more influence and control over the outcomes in your life than you do yourself, you will be more vulnerable to their influence and to their attempts at manipulation. Moreover, to the extent that you collude with or become victim to their manipulation, your sense of being controlled by forces outside yourself will be reinforced and perpetuated.

By developing an internal LOC and a higher sense of personal efficacy, you will be less subject to manipulators. And in turn, by making yourself a harder target for manipulators, you will increase your sense of controlling your own outcomes in life.

When you have the perception and expectation that your outcomes in life are largely out of your own control and therefore under the control of other people and/or other out-side forces more powerful than yourself, you also will be more likely to experience depression.

The connection between an external LOC and depression lies in the construct of *learned helplessness*—the mind-set that negative things do and will happen to you of significant consequence *and* that there is very little to nothing that you can do to affect or change those events. When you believe that bad things *will* happen and that your own actions are essentially futile to control, predict, prevent, minimize, or escape from those negative outcomes, you have the mind-set that *is* depression.

An external LOC therefore makes you vulnerable to depression, which, in turn, saps whatever drive, energy, and optimism you may have left to try to make things different in your life. Clearly, this is a vicious cycle. An external LOC also can affect your physical health because the "giving in/given up" mind-set is a known risk factor in lowering immune responses and compromising overall health.

People with an internal LOC are less likely to develop depression because, by definition, they do not subscribe to the learned helplessness mind-set. They believe that what they do does make a difference—a big one—in the things that happen to them in life.

Now you know the buttons manipulators push—the seven areas of personality that make you vulnerable to manipulation. Later you will learn how to strengthen and correct your thinking in these areas of vulnerability in order to lower your susceptibility to manipulators.

In Chapter 5 we will take a look at what drives manipulators to push other people around.

5

Manipulators' Motives

NOW THAT YOU KNOW how manipulators push your "buttons," let's turn the tables by examining the typical motives of manipulators. This is one way to help level the playing field between you and those who manipulate you. After all, if the buttons that you show to the outside world mark you as an easy target for manipulation, shouldn't you learn to spot a manipulator by identifying his or her motives? In so doing, you may be able to head off a manipulative relationship before it gets going.

However, spotting a manipulator is not always easy. Even if you are "on" to his or her motives, there are obstacles. Recognize, for example, that part of the skilled manipulator's presentation is that he often covers or disguises his motives from others. He may be quite intentional about doing so by deliberately misrepresenting his reasons for saying or doing certain things in relationships with others that are, at their core, manipulative in nature.

Sometimes manipulators may even lie to themselves about their true underlying motives. This increases the difficulty of exposing a manipulator. It is one thing to uncover manipulators who lie to you; but when they lie to themselves, it makes the lies they tell you more believable or credible.

Regardless of whether a manipulator is conscious or intentional about his motives or not, the negative impact on the target or victim is essentially the same.

What Makes Manipulators Do What They Do?

Manipulation exists because it works. The best way to stop a manipulator is simply to disable her tactics—make her manipulation ineffective because you stop complying with her demands, desires, requests, or subtle or overt pressure.

When manipulative tactics stop being effective in advancing the ends of the manipulator—when you stop being a mark and transform yourself into a harder target for manipulators—the manipulator's tactics likely will change. Quite possibly, the manipulator will disengage from the relationship altogether and seek a new mark or victim. Manipulators can be compared with water running downhill, always seeking the path of least resistance.

The reason is not any more complicated than this: Manipulators do not want to have *to work* at manipulating. It comes easily and naturally to them. They do it because it is easy—because you make it easy.

The purpose of this chapter is not to enlighten manipulators. I do not expect manipulators to be interested in reading this book. Moreover, I do not delude myself into thinking that if manipulators only knew the harm they did, they would have an "Ah-hah!" moment of insight and decide to change their ways. I know better. And you shouldn't delude yourself either.

Instead, my purpose is to describe the motives and mind-sets of manipulators so that you have a better understanding of what you are up against. By increasing your understanding of what makes manipulators behave as they do, you will have a better understanding of why you feel so confused, violated, unhappy, demeaned, and otherwise diminished in your relationships with manipulative people.

Basic Rules of Manipulation

Keep these key points foremost in your mind:

- You cannot and will not outmanipulate a skilled manipulator; do not even try.
- Always pay attention to what the manipulator does, not what he or she says.
- Do not inquire why he or she is behaving in a particular way and expect to get a valid, useful, or truthful answer. Remember, "Why" is a luxury question. Do not bother asking the question; when you finish this book, you will know the answer. Just because a manipulator denies being manipulative or disguises his or her motives verbally does not mean that you are wrong in your identification. Do not expect the manipulator to give you an honest answer.
- You cannot and will not change a manipulator by pointing out his or her shortcomings.
- Do not bother telling a manipulator that she is not being fair or kind or loving. If your purpose in doing so is to effect change, forget it; it simply will not happen.
- You cannot appeal to a manipulator's empathy with your feelings. Do not imagine that by telling him how you *feel* as the victim of manipulation you will accomplish anything. The manipulator does not care; he most likely is incapable of empathy altogether.

- The *only* effective way to change a manipulator is to make her tactics ineffective by changing yourself. You will not change the manipulator, but you can change the manipulative relationship. When you stop rewarding manipulative tactics by ceasing to cooperate, comply, please, or acquiesce, you will necessarily alter the nature and the dynamics of the manipulative relationship. Remember, if manipulation turns out to be hard work, the manipulator will likely give up.
- Do not put your energy into making the manipulator more aware of your feelings or more aware of her motives. This only empowers her. Instead, put your energy into raising your own level of awareness and into changing your behavior so that you do not fall into your familiar victim patterns and roles.

Manipulative Motives

Manipulators operate out of three principal interpersonal motives:

1. They need to advance their own purposes and their own personal gain at virtually any cost to others. They are entirely self-serving and selfish by disposition, even if they say otherwise. Remember, smart, skilled manipulators know how to disguise their motives, sometimes even to themselves.

   Just because a manipulator tells you that he is doing something for your own good—or telling you something because he cares enough to be "totally honest" and he says that he has your very best interests at heart—*do not believe it*. Good lip service is part of the manipulator's tactics.

Why do manipulative people often represent themselves as concerned about others, as unselfish and altruistic? *Because it works.* Remember, the manipulator will say and do whatever is necessary to advance his own ends, purposes, or personal gain. This includes saying that he believes himself to be a good, kind, fair-minded, honest, and generous person. His tactics even may include making you feel guilty or like an unfair, mean-spirited, distrusting, and generally bad person for suspecting that he is operating out of manipulative motives.

2. The manipulator has strong needs to attain feelings of power and superiority in relationships with other people. She wants the control she seeks over others to be acknowledged and validated. The victim's compliance with manipulative tactics is the acknowledgment and validation the manipulator seeks.

   Paradoxically, this need springs from strong underlying—sometimes unconscious—feelings of inferiority and low self-esteem. The manipulator's low self-esteem is frequently hidden by outward layers of personality style and presentation characterized by what looks like bold self-confidence and even an inflated or grandiose ego or sense of self. This is the paradox of the manipulative personality: She operates out of low self-esteem but with an inflated or strong-appearing sense of self-confidence.

   In fact, the manipulator's strong need to exert and demonstrate power and control over others arises from the underlying strong need to compensate for feelings of inferiority and inadequacy. The manipulator, who has contempt for people like herself, consciously rejects these weak feelings.

The manipulator views power as finite. In other words, there is not enough power to go around for her to share or to acknowledge and respect your right to be empowered to make decisions and to attain control in your own life. If you are empowered to *any* degree, this represents less power for her.

The manipulator views power as a zero-sum game. This means that there is always someone who wins by attaining, maintaining, and exercising power and control over others, and there is always someone who loses by ceding control to the winner. There is no room in the manipulator's model of human relationships for a win-win scenario where power is shared or where everyone comes out gaining or benefiting from a given interaction.

If you attempt to exercise power and control—even if it is just over your own decisions and behavior—the manipulator will feel threatened because she needs all the power that is around to get. If you exercise power in your own life, then from the manipulator's standpoint, you are taking power away from her. She therefore will feel compelled to take immediate retaliatory steps to regain control.

3. Manipulators want and need to feel *in control*. Feeling like they are out of control or that they might even be losing control in any realm evokes very high levels of anxiety. The manipulator's need to feel in control extends beyond his or her desires or needs to control others. Manipulators want to be seen and want to see themselves as being in control of their emotions, especially emotions that they associate with weakness, such as anxiety, sadness, or loneli-

ness. In competitive situations, they want to win—
at nearly any cost to others.

While manipulators have a strong, even pathologic
or sick need to control others, they generally struggle
with control issues in their own lives. Their need to
maintain control over others is frequently manifested
by a need to "be right" and to make others "wrong."
There is no room in the manipulator's mind for both
people in a given argument or conflict in which he is
involved to each have valid positions, nor is their room
for two different and equally "right," albeit separate,
points of view. For the manipulator, *only one person
can be right*—and that must be him. The other person
necessarily becomes wrong to the extent that there is
less than full agreement with the manipulator.

The need of manipulators to control others is closely allied
to their need *to feel in control*—not only of others but of
themselves as well. Manipulative people frequently suffer
from feelings of high anxiety when their control is threatened.
Since they cannot easily or gracefully cede control to others,
they will tend to over- or micromanage in business situations.
Manipulators typically oversupervise delegated tasks in business or domestic or personal situations. Because control is
such a big issue, manipulators tend to dislike any situation
that involves ambiguity. They like to think in black and white,
either/or terms. Gray areas make them nervous.

In contradiction, however, their control issues sometimes
reveal themselves as problems maintaining control over certain areas of their *own* behavior. Because control is a central
psychological issue for manipulators, they may exhibit control problems by loss of control in these areas:

- Anger
- Food consumption/weight control
- Alcohol consumption
- Drug use
- Cigarette use
- Overcontrolled or undercontrolled signs of emotionality and mood variations

Do Manipulators Understand Their Own Motives?

Not necessarily. Manipulators generally can be categorized into two groups: those who are aware and conscious of their manipulative motives and goals and those who remain largely unconscious or unaware of the manipulative methods they employ in their relationships with others. As we will see in Chapter 6, people with overt, aggressive, controlling personalities are far easier to identify as manipulative than those whose styles are more covert.

The reason most people ask questions about manipulators' awareness of their motives concerns their capacity or willingness to change. To nonmanipulative people, making another person conscious or aware that he is violating the rights of others by trying to manipulate them should be sufficient to make them change. Not so.

The degree of a manipulator's awareness does have some bearing on his or her ability or willingness to change. Manipulators who are self-aware and intentional about being manipulative are least likely to change. In psychological terms, their manipulation is *ego-congruent,* a term that means that being manipulative and controlling of others fits with the way they think consciously of themselves. In other words, they do not experience inner conflict or turmoil over the thought that their behavior may violate the rights of others. They do not care, or they have rationalized their behavior to the point that they may believe that they are doing what is good or right for others anyway.

When manipulation is ego-congruent and when it is effective (i.e., it works to get the manipulator what she wants), there is little motivation for change. Although nonmanipulative people may find it surprising, merely pointing out to a conscious manipulator that his tactics are manipulative or exploitative of the rights of others creates little to no incentive to change. In fact, for such people, change is entirely instrumental—meaning that they will change their tactics only when the manipulation no longer accomplishes their ends or purposes. Only when manipulation is no longer effective in eliciting and controlling the behavior of others so as to serve to advance the manipulator's interests and personal gain is change even a possibility.

Under such circumstances, when manipulation stops working, the manipulator may switch or shift tactics. However, do not expect a realignment or breakthrough in the fundamental structure of her personality or values. This kind of change is not borne of insight and/or a desire to be a better or healthier person. Remember, most manipulators will go to great lengths to avoid looking inside too deeply because this tends to be very anxiety provoking.

For ego-congruent manipulators, change is borne of a shift in outcomes rather than an increase in insight. And if and when manipulation begins working again—or when the shift has merely been to other more effective forms of manipulation—the manipulation will be reestablished.

The second group of manipulators tends to be far less conscious and self-aware of the nature of their control of other people. These manipulators often evolve their tactics defensively as a way to deal with their own anxieties and fears. For many of these people, being seen as a manipulator is *ego-incongruent,* or inconsistent and at odds with the view they hold of themselves. Thus, when an ego-incongruent manipulator is confronted with exposure of his manipulation, there may be enough inner conflict generated to help motivate change. However, because manipulators typically are low on empathy—or lack the capacity altogether to feel as others feel—the insight that their behavior is hurting another person generally is not sufficient to tip the scales toward change.

Instead, the insight needs to be coupled with the development of alternative methods or different tactics. Again, the big leverage with *both* conscious and unconscious manipulators is to change the effectiveness of their tactics. Manipulators may change their tactics when their methods stop working to advance their ends, or they may opt out of the relationship altogether, seeking another venue in which their manipulative methods do work.

Thus the bottom line remains the same: *The best way to change a manipulator is to change your own behavior.* When you stop rewarding the manipulation by giving in and by giving the manipulator what he or she wants—*power and control*—you will set the wheels of change in motion.

When you are involved with a manipulative person, do not expect that person necessarily to admit to using manipulative tactics or purposes. Patients in therapy are often trapped by their own mistaken and naive thinking that other people always mean what they say. Just because a manipulator denies being manipulative does not mean that he or she is not being exactly that. In fact, the denial itself is a chief component of the ongoing manipulation.

Remember my advice earlier: Always pay attention to what the manipulator *does*, not what he or she *says*.

What You Can Expect

Keep in mind that manipulators of both types seldom admit to their manipulation easily or in an up-front or direct way. They tend to keep their manipulative motivation under wraps for several reasons.

First, manipulation generally is not viewed as a desirable or acceptable tactic to use interpersonally. Because it is discouraged and/or regarded negatively, skilled manipulators tend to keep their motives covert. They prefer to cloak their motives in guises that are more socially acceptable, such as:

- *Love and caring:* "I'm doing this out of care/love for you."
- *Expertise:* "I'm telling you this because I've had way more experience in these matters, and I know better."
- *Altruism and generosity:* "I'm doing this for your own good, even though it doesn't benefit me."
- *Role endowment:* "I'm telling you what to do because that is my role/obligation."

Second, as stated earlier, sometimes manipulators keep their true motives hidden even from themselves. In the face of confrontation concerning their manipulation, they often will use denial as a defense mechanism. Introspection and self-examination are, at best, only superficial with most manipulators, as too much light shining on their underlying motives will tend to make them anxious, defensive, and often angry. While manipulators tend to act deliberately—with end goals in mind—they do not generally require themselves to act out of a sense of moral intention or out of a personal code or value system of right and wrong or good and bad behavior and treatment of others. Instead, they act out of a sense of what works to advance their own ends.

Third and most obvious, manipulators lie. It is one of their most effective tactics. If it suits the ends of a manipulator to make you think that he is *not* manipulating, he will do whatever is necessary to disabuse you of even your slightest suspicions, let alone your outright accusations or confrontations. Skilled manipulators are adept at making their accusers (or anyone who even suggests that they may be manipulating) feel guilty and ill-mannered for even questioning their motives.

How Manipulators Look at the World

First, it is important to accept that manipulators look at the world in a different way than nonmanipulators. And in some critical ways, their worldview determines their behavior, which, in a cyclic turn, helps to validate their view of the world in the first place. As mentioned earlier, manipulators see the world in general in black and white, either/or terms, especially with respect to manipulation: Their view is that either you play or you get played.

In other words, manipulators believe that there are only two roles in relationships—you are either manipulated (the victim), or you are the manipulator (in their view, the one in power and control). Manipulators see no other way that relationships operate. They cannot envision participating in a relationship between equals, for example. Such a relationship is beyond their understanding and comprehension.

They simply cannot imagine their role in a mutually inter-dependent relationship in which there is balanced decision making and shared control and in which the rights of both parties to make critical decisions about their own lives are acknowledged and respected by both participants. They cannot imagine trusting someone else enough to make such a shared and balanced relationship possible, and they fundamentally do not see themselves as trustworthy in the sense that another person could really trust them to respect and protect the rights of both.

Second, because manipulators see life as a zero-sum game, in almost every important dimension—which to a manipulator primarily comprises power, control, and superiority—the manipulator believes that there are winners and losers. In a two-person relationship, someone must win, and someone must lose. It is not complicated math. There is no room for a win-win or a lose-lose scenario. In any interpersonal setting, the manipulator believes that if she gives something to the other person—or allows the other person to claim or attain something the manipulator values—the pot is diminished, and there is necessarily less for her. This view, of course, gives rise to competition, rivalry, and jealousy—toxic emotions that taint and compromise the quality of manipulators' relationships.

The third element of the manipulator's worldview is that other people exist to serve or meet his needs. This allows for no exercise of *empathy*—the ability to feel as another person feels. In fact, there are many manipulators (as we will see in Chapter 6) who lack the capacity for empathy altogether. They literally cannot fathom that there even *is* another way to feel or think or need other than that arising from their own perspective.

The fourth element of the manipulator's worldview, closely related to the third, is a huge sense of entitlement. The manipulator operates from the viewpoint, consciously or unconsciously, that he *deserves* to have his needs met and purposes served. He may believe that this is true because of a bad childhood or other negative life experiences in which the manipulator perceives that other people (or life in general) wounded him in some important way; therefore, the world *owes* him back. Life becomes about evening up the score and making sure that he does not get cheated, mistreated, hurt, damaged, short-changed, or otherwise injured in any way. The manipulator who operates out of this mind-set of entitlement believes that he is *special* and therefore merits special compliance from others. It is difficult for the manipulator to grasp the concept of violating the rights of others because (1) he cannot really *feel* that others have rights of their own and (2) he is *entitled* to have other people subordinate their needs to his.

How Manipulators Create the World They Perceive

The fifth element of the manipulator's worldview merits special consideration here because of the unique way in which this perception transforms into a self-fulfilling prophecy. The manipulator uses the defense mechanism of *projection* in his dealings with the world of others.

She believes that given a choice, everyone else believes the same way she does. In other words, other people see the world in the same stark win-lose terms. She feels that others also believe that they can play or they will get played—and that given a choice, others will always opt for being the controlling/manipulating party. She feels that others only feel their own needs—which the manipulator can barely imagine as being different fundamentally from her own. And finally, she feels that others share in her self-centered sense of entitlement.

Given this tendency toward projection—toward seeing in the motives and beliefs of others the same drives that propel her interpersonal dealings—the manipulator cannot act in a trusting manner. She instinctively will approach any situation that requires a choice between trusting another person and behaving cooperatively versus not trusting another person and behaving competitively by opting for the latter strategy.

The manipulator always will put the distrusting foot forward; because she expects others to act only out of competitive self-interest, she will make the preemptive competitive strike first.

The Prisoner's Dilemma

A classic social psychology study demonstrates the self-fulfilling prophecy impact of this interpersonal strategy. It is a match called the *prisoner's dilemma game* in which two people play, and it is sometimes referred to as a *game of social domination*.

The late, great mathematician Albert W. Tucker developed the game in 1950. In his original game, he conceived the story of two burglars, Bob and Al. The two crooks are captured near the scene of a crime and are taken to police headquarters, where they are split up and placed in separate cells and interrogated. The police tell each of them that things will go easier on them if they confess. Will it?

Each prisoner now has to decide whether or not to confess and implicate his pal. The police tell them that if *neither* man confesses, they will *both* go to prison for a year anyway on a charge of carrying a concealed weapon. If each of them confesses and implicates the other, then each will go to prison for 10 years. But if only one confesses and implicates the other, then the one who confessed will go free, and the other will serve the maximum sentence of 20 years. How do they decide?

There are only two possible strategies: confess or don't confess. No other option is available. In the following matrix first developed by Tucker, known as the *prisoner's dilemma matrix* or *payoff,* you can see the options open to each prisoner and the consequences of each decision when viewed against the decision of the other prisoner.

Bob's possible consequences are to the left of the comma in each square of the grid, whereas Al's are to the right. If Al and Bob both confess and implicate the other, they each get 10 years. If Al and Bob both clam up, they each get 1 year. However if Al confesses and implicates Bob and Bob does not confess, Al goes free and Bob gets 20 years. And if the reverse

Original Prisoner's Dilemma Matrix

		Al	
		Confess	Don't confess
Bob	Confess	10, 10 years	20, 0 years
	Don't confess	20, 0 years	1, 1 year

is true, where Bob confesses and Al does not, then Bob gets 20 years and Al goes free.

Over the years, many variations of the prisoner's dilemma have been conceived to look at how people cooperate or do not cooperate in social settings. We can view manipulators through the same prism.

In one variation, the matrix labels are changed from "confess/don't confess" to "cooperate/compete." The game is sometimes played by awarding gold coins or dollars, depending on the outcome of each move.

Each person, on any given move, can play to cooperate or to compete. In the game's setup, if both people cooperate on the same move, they both win moderate outcomes ($10). However, if one person cooperates while the other person competes, the cooperator loses (earns $0); conversely, the competitor wins big ($20.) This is the zero-sum outcome—one winner and one loser. Finally, if both parties choose to compete, they each get only a small win ($1).

A true manipulator will always look at the game by assuming that the person he or she is playing against will compete. Competing is the manipulator's natural mind-set.

Variation of The Prisoner's Dilemma Matrix

		Al	
		Cooperate	Compete
Bob	Cooperate	$10, $10	$0, $20
	Compete	$20, $0	$1, $1

However, when you ponder the game, you will realize that the best strategy to maximize both parties' outcomes is for them to trust each other to cooperate on every move. If both cooperate, each earns $10 for each move. However, the risk involved is that if you choose to cooperate and the other player competes, you get zero and your opponent wins $20.

People who play with the manipulator's mind-set believe that everyone will automatically play to win—or to maximize gain and minimize loss on each turn—by playing competitively. However, this option will only work best for the competitive player when the opponent plays cooperatively: The competitor gets $20, and the cooperator gets $0.

Manipulators always play the competitive move. When they first sit down to play with an opponent, they make the competitive move. Sometimes their opponent will make a cooperative move on the first try; sometimes he will not. However, given that *the manipulator continues to play competitively*, the originally cooperative opponent has no choice but to *change his tactics* into also being a nontrusting competitor. In this way, the opponent will improve his score by $1 (up from $0) and in so doing also reduce the manipulator's score to $1.

On the other hand, consider the experience of people who examine the matrix and choose on their first move to play cooperatively, *trusting* the other player to also cooperate so that each gets $10 on every move. If both players do play cooperatively, over 10 moves, each will accrue $100. As long as both players continue to play cooperatively—that is, by trusting one another—their gain will be guaranteed over the course of the game.

However, if a cooperative person gets burned by a competitive person on the first few rounds, the only option open to the trusting person is to switch strategies and become competitive too—just as a defense.

Studies of behavior in the prisoner's dilemma game show that cooperators have varied experiences playing the game. Sometimes they meet other cooperators and both walk away happy. At other times, though, they meet competitors whose distrustful, self-aggrandizing strategy makes the cooperator shift by necessity to a competitive strategy as a defense. Very few people will continue to play cooperatively throughout the game when faced with a competitor. When asked to summarize their feelings after several rounds playing different people, the cooperators may shrug their shoulders and say that it is just like life: There are all different sorts of people.

On the other hand, competitive players almost always wind up having the experience that both players compete in the game. Because the competitive (manipulative) player converts his opponent to a competitive strategy (but will not allow himself to be similarly converted to a cooperative strategy because cooperation requires interpersonal trust), his experience with others is not varied. His own behavior *creates* competition in others and thereby validates his original view that others are not to be trusted.

Using the prisoner's dilemma game as a model for life, you can readily see that manipulators who inherently distrust others and project their own competitive impulses on others actually will *create* the very social world they imagine. Their life experience will wind up confirming their belief system, although they typically do not understand how their own distrusting behavior creates distrust, competition, and rivalry in others.

The pattern captured by the essence of the gaming model shows how and why manipulators rationalize their view that life is a dog-eat-dog game where each person must do what is necessary to advance his own personal needs even if it is at the expense of others. Manipulators believe that this behavior is justified because they believe that other people will do the same to them.

Think how this mind-set can affect and poison an interpersonal relationship. Trusting people who allow for the possibility that others can, on occasion, choose to behave altruistically and/or generously or, as in the prisoner's dilemma game, others can choose to cooperate because it is rational and adaptive will be *open* to the possibility of trusting relationships. If you approach the world with an open but realistic attitude that allows for both kinds of people—trusting souls and self-promoting competitors—your experiences will mirror your expectations. You likely will meet both kinds of people and have the opportunity to form relationships in which mutual trust and cooperation exist and are cherished by both participants.

In cooperation and trust lies the context for mutual respect and healthy interdependence—the blend of autonomy and interdependence that makes intimacy, high self-esteem, strong sense of self, and solid self-reliance possible.

However, the realistic cooperator also knows that competitive manipulators exist in the world; when the competitive opponent is met, the cooperator can adjust and adapt his or her behavior accordingly. You do not have to reward manipulators by allowing their exploitative behavior and tactics to work.

Summary

Manipulation derives from a mind-set and worldview that allows it to be rationalized or denied. Trying to get a manipulator to change by setting a good example and allowing yourself to be exploited only rewards his or her manipulative tactics.

The best chance you have to change a manipulator is to stop rewarding her tactics. Manipulation persists because it works. It is effective. As long as a manipulator gets you to comply with her needs and give in to her control, she will continue to relate to you in a manipulative fashion.

To change a manipulator, you must change your own behavior. The manipulator wants to advance her personal gain and self-interest and simply does not care if this happens at the expense of your interests, well-being, peace of mind, or psychological or physical health. When you learn to block her tactics effectively with moves of your own—which you will learn as you continue to read this book—you will block the manipulator and gradually stop allowing yourself to be manipulated.

When her manipulation stops working, the manipulator's self-interest will be better served by switching methods or—*and you must accept this possibility at the outset*—by switching relationships altogether. Blocking the manipulator's tactics may not result in losing the relationship. However, you must confront this possibility in order to embrace your freedom and to find the way out of the destructive pattern of exploitation and manipulation in which you may be enmeshed. If you are not willing to lose the relationship—even when it means losing yourself in the process—*then you are not ready to stop being a victim.*

Finally, people are not always consistent with respect to the role they play in relationships. Many manipulators have learned their craft of control from participation in relationships in which they were the victims. Sometimes people who have been subject to aversive manipulation in one relationship vow to never be in the victim role again; instead, they successfully position themselves to be the manipulator in their next relationship.

In this chapter you have learned more about what drives manipulators. In Chapter 6 we will take a look at the typical or most common personality styles of manipulative people. In other words, who are the usual suspects?

6

Who Are the Manipulators in Your Life?

NEARLY EVERY RELATIONSHIP includes the occasional use of influence or persuasion. This is to be expected. These efforts may be as mundane as a husband trying to sway his wife's dining preference to his favorite restaurant or a wife attempting to persuade her husband to see the movie of her choice. On the other hand, the tactics of influence may become intensified and even coercive, rising to the level of emotional blackmail. The boyfriend who threatens to break up—or emotionally abandon—his girlfriend unless she complies with his every sexual proclivity is one example of toxic influence tactics—a particularly loathsome form of manipulation.

Manipulation, then, is a subcategory of what psychologists broadly call *social influence*—in other words, the ways in which people try to intentionally change one another. There is nothing inherently wrong with or unhealthy about attempts to influence people. Doctors, for example, seek to change our health habits. Good teachers use tactics of persuasion (and sometimes bribery in the form of candy) to motivate and stimulate their students. Parents exert their influence over their children as often as necessary, as they should. Indeed, raising and guiding children is very largely a process of cumulative influence over many years.

However, there are boundaries to everything, and there are healthy or appropriate limits. Determination of what constitutes healthy social *influence* versus unhealthy *manipulation* depends primarily on the motives and attitude of the influencer toward his or her target or mark and secondarily on the tactics used in the attempt to change behavior or to alter the other's thoughts and feelings.

If the influencer recognizes and respects the personal integrity and rights of others—including the right of others to choose *not* to go along with the persuasion—and if he or she uses tactics that are appropriately mature and respectful of all parties concerned, the influence is likely to fall somewhere within the range of benign or harmless to benevolent and altruistic. However, once the motive turns to exploitation and the tactics become coercive, the line is crossed from influence to manipulation.

And this is where trouble begins.

Crossing the Line

In the psychological lexicon, the term *manipulation* has a derogatory and negative connotation or meaning. After all, when was the last time you heard anyone referred to in a positive way with the noun *manipulator*? Try to imagine a conversation between two women, with one trying to fix up the other on a blind date, that sounds like this:

"Oh, you'll just love Bob."

"What's he like?"

"He's tall, handsome, loves to dance, and is a great manipulator."

Generally, *manipulation* refers to attempts to change
another person using methods that are exploitative, devious,
deceptive, insidious, or unfair. And, manipulation is *always*
one-sided, asymmetrical, or unbalanced in its motivation.
Manipulation advances the interests and furthers the goals of
the manipulator only, without regard to the needs or interests
of the mark—and often at the mark's expense.

Once the line between appropriate influence and manipulation is crossed, relationships become disturbed and troubled.

Thus, while virtually all people attempt to influence others
to one extent or another, individuals differ with respect to
whether or not they use tactics of manipulation as a consistent
style in their interpersonal relationships. In fact, the tendency to
cross the line from respectful influence to outright exploitation
and disregard for the rights of others is a defining feature—and
an important diagnostic criterion—of unhealthy personality
functioning.

Simply put, *personality* is the name psychologists give to
the enduring pattern of thoughts, behaviors, and feelings that
characterizes each individual. In a sense, each of us has a kind
of personality "fingerprint" that derives about half from
genetic programming and half from environmental influences,
a roughly 50:50 nature/nurture split.

In Chapters 3 and 4 you had an opportunity to examine
and better understand those aspects of your own personality
that make you vulnerable to the pressure tactics of manipulation in your life. Later in this book you will learn strategies

to resist the tactics of manipulation so that you may develop a better sense of control over your own behavior, thoughts, and feelings—in short, over the way your life is going and over the way things either work out for you or do not.

Building effective resistance strategies, however, depends first on your being able to recognize *when*, *how*, and *by whom* you are being manipulated. It is important for you to have a clear, unambiguous understanding of who is manipulating you—and that you are, in fact, being manipulated.

Identifying manipulators in your life is not always an easy task. As I have warned, skilled manipulators include as part of their core repertoire keeping you off balance, confused, and eventually doubtful of your own perceptions and judgments. With adequate training and practice, however, you can and will learn to pick up manipulators on your psychological radar screen, even if they are operating at stealth frequencies.

The evidence of manipulation can be detected in three primary areas: (1) in the personality of the manipulator, (2) in the negative emotional impact the aversive control of the manipulator is exerting on you, and (3) on the dynamics of the relationship itself—that is, how the relationship works or fails to work as a source of satisfaction and/or gratification for either one or both of the participants.

As I mentioned before, no one is fully immune to being manipulated. Similarly, each of us is capable of manipulating (or at least trying to manipulate) others. However, certain discrete personality types are likely to engage in manipulation more consistently than others. Moreover, individuals who fall into one or more of the personality patterns outlined below will be likely to use manipulative tactics across a range of different relationships (e.g., familial, work, and so on) and across various situations and/or periods of time.

Direct Control versus Evocation

As nearly anyone who has been personally involved with, related to, or worked for or with a manipulative personality will attest, the dominant themes of the relationship become issues of power and control, imbalance or unfairness, exploitation, and inability or unwillingness to change. However, while involvement with all manipulators yields parallel experiences for their marks, the specific personality traits of the manipulator play a key role in determining which tactics are used to manipulate others (e.g., charm, whining, the silent treatment, and so on). Chapter 7 will explore the issue of the *tactics of manipulation.*

Various personality types that use manipulation also may differ with respect to how intentional or aware they actually are of their impact on others. As you will see, some personality types are very conscious and intentional about their purposes. Without apology and with near-total disregard for the integrity or rights of others, these willful manipulators will do whatever they believe is necessary to advance their own self-interest. Simply put, these manipulative personalities seek to gain their way with others by applying *direct control.*

For example, a boss who overtly manipulates subordinates to do certain things is applying direct control. In this case, the manipulation is easy to spot. However, other personality types manipulate others through less conscious or intentional means. Instead, aspects of the manipulator's typically rigid and inflexible personality traits cause others to react in negative, undesired ways. In this sense, the manipulator controls the emotional and behavioral reactions of the mark through *evocation.* This means that his or her traits or actions *evoke* predictable reactions in others.

Simply stated, people with hostile, aggressive personalities *expect* others to be hostile. Consequently, they treat other people aggressively. When people are treated aggressively, they tend to exhibit hostility in return. Thus, since hostility breeds hostility, an aggressive person often evokes hostility from others.

From the perspective of the mark, his or her hostile, angry response is *manipulated* (evoked) by the initial aggression. Married couples or couples in long relationships, for example, are particularly adept at evoking anger or upset in their partners by performing certain actions, even if they are not always conscious or aware of it. The husband who yells at his wife because he feels stressed and pressured may consistently evoke a tearful emotional response that, in turn, evokes feelings of guilt and resentment in him. Or the wife who denigrates her husband for being a poor lover may well evoke even greater sexual performance anxiety that will indeed confirm her (and his) worst fears.

Recall Cindy and Bob, the first of the five acts in Chapter 2. Cindy manipulates reactions in Bob—anxiety, stomach pains, guilt—through evocation.

Manipulating Your Life: The Usual Suspects

While anyone can employ manipulative tactics once in a while, certain personality types are, by definition, inclined to use manipulation as a consistent method of interpersonal influence and control. This is especially true of those who see how manipulation has worked to their advantage in the past and consider it an easy way to get what they want.

Learning about these personality types will help you to recognize individuals who are likely to engage in manipulative behavior. In addition to sensitizing you to certain types of manipulators, your newfound knowledge will enable you to avoid such people and shield yourself from falling victim to their insidious traps.

Training yourself to identify the personality styles described below is the first step in the vital process of self-protection. Remember, your goal is not to directly *change* those who now attempt and/or succeed at manipulating you. Do not even try; it is pointless. After all, it is unlikely that you will become more adept at manipulating than a skilled and experienced manipulator, and this is not our goal. However, once you have identified the problem—that is, that *you* are the mark of a manipulator and, as such, are at risk yourself of losing vital self-esteem, diminishing your sense of control over your feelings, thoughts, and actions, and compromising your overall well-being and happiness—you will be in a position to foil the manipulator by *not complying with or capitulating to* his or her exploitative purposes, desires, or schemes.

When manipulation stops working—because *you* cease to reward it with compliance and *you* stop colluding with the manipulator's hidden or open agenda—the manipulator will, of necessity, alter his or her tactics or, if possible, move on to another mark. Remember, manipulators do not want to break a sweat; they always seek the path of *least* resistance.

Spotting Manipulators in Your Midst

Think of this chapter as a kind of field guide to manipulators in their natural habitat. I will describe for you the essential personality traits and styles of several types of manipulative personalities.

Who are the usual suspects? And where is their natural habitat? The answer to the second question is that manipulators exist within your life space—that is, they are among the people with whom you interact on a regular basis, people with whom you are involved in relationships ranging from very close, intimate bonds to more formal or structured relationships such as those which exist at work.

While manipulation can occur in virtually any relationship, the individuals who can exert the greatest impact on your sense of identity, security, status, self-worth, and sense of personal adequacy are also the very ones who have a high potential for manipulation. This is so because such relationships provide a context in which you have both the most to *gain* and/or the most to *lose* from the outcomes or ways in which the relationships function. This is a hard pill to swallow: The manipulators in your midst *may* be among those people with whom you interact on an up close and personal basis, including:

- Family members
- Marriage partners
- Romantic/sexual relationships
- Work relationships—with superiors, coworkers, and subordinates
- Friendships
- Academic relationships—especially with superiors
- Professional relationships—such as those with doctors, lawyers, and therapists

I am certainly not saying that everyone or mostly everyone in your life is manipulating you—although it sometimes may feel that way. Nor am I advising you to keep people at arm's length or to shut out close or intimate relationships from your life. On the contrary! It is only from healthy close relationships that our most important needs for love, connection, meaning, and security are met.

However, whether your relationships are helping you or hurting you depends on whether you and the people with whom you relate are capable of maintaining balanced relationships that acknowledge and respect the personal rights and integrity of everyone concerned. And this, of course, requires that you be psychologically healthy yourself and that you are involved with people who have essentially healthy, nonmanipulative personalities.

Now this is a pretty tall order, isn't it? Particularly because you cannot always control or choose the people with whom you must relate. You cannot pick your family. You are likely to have little control over the selection of coworkers or the people to whom you report at work and who therefore exercise control over vital aspects of your career and financial security.

The fact is that I do not know anyone who doesn't have at least one story to tell about a relationship—be it personal or business, family or friend—in which they found themselves enmeshed with and manipulated by an individual who had major personality problems.

The reality is that there *are* big-time manipulators who, at one point or another, are likely to enter or reveal themselves within your life space. The best protection you have is to sharpen your recognition skills—the sooner you can accurately spot a likely manipulator, the better prepared you will be to make yourself a hardened and less vulnerable target, able to resist even the cagiest manipulative tactics.

Remember, all of us are capable of both being a manipulator and being used or exploited by one. However, there are some personality types that are far more likely than others to use manipulation in their relationships. It is important for us to identify and discuss the profile of these *manipulative personalities.*

Three Important Goals

My purpose in this chapter is threefold. First is to help you to achieve greater understanding, insight, and clarity about the relationships in which you are involved and, in particular, about the dynamics of power and control that characterize those relationships. Over time, participation in a manipulative relationship as the mark or target produces a sense of loss of control—over your actions, your behavior, and even your thoughts and feelings. Accompanying this loss of control is a distressing sense of confusion, discomfort, and lack of clarity about the motives and actions of the manipulator. Ironically, the more skilled and effective the manipulator, the more confused and unclear you are likely to feel about when, how, and even *if* you are, in fact, being manipulated.

All too often the mark seeks to clarify what is going on by asking the manipulator to clarify his motives. However, you must remember that skilled manipulators frequently and convincingly lie and deny their motives, intentions, or goals when confronted directly. Thus the clarification the mark naively seeks from a manipulator—the admission that manipulation is indeed occurring—remains elusive.

As you will soon learn, personalities who manipulate by *evoking* certain undesirable reactions in others are even less likely to admit to their manipulative tactics or goals because they are generally unaware of the impact of their behavior on others. You cannot rely on the manipulator to identify and clarify her motives and goals. To do so is merely to play even further into the manipulation. However, this does not mean that you must or should remain unclear about whether and how you are colluding—albeit unintentionally—in a manipulative relationship. It does mean that the responsibility for figuring out what is going on and, more important, for stopping the manipulation by rendering it ineffective must rest with *you*. You are on your own in this sense, since your manipulative partner is the last person who would—even if she could—help you out.

As long as you remain in a foggy psychological state about how the relationship operates, the more control you will yield over your actions, thoughts, and feelings *and* the less effective you will become to successfully resist the insidious influence of the manipulator. A foggy psychological state is very much like driving a car in foggy conditions. Can you do it? Yes. Is it safe? No. For your own protection, it is essential to clear the fog in your mind.

The second purpose, then, is to help you to develop identification and recognition skills. In other words, by learning to recognize the personality traits and styles of people who are likely to use manipulation as a customary practice in their relationships, you will arm yourself with an early warning system. Once you recognize that manipulation *might* occur, you can plan a resistance strategy that will preserve and protect your boundaries, choices, and individual freedom if indeed manipulation does begin.

And the third purpose is to focus the aim of your efforts *on yourself* rather than on the manipulator. My intention in providing the descriptions that follow is neither to turn you into a diagnostician nor to suggest that, once a manipulator is identified, you embark on a "treatment" strategy in which you try to *change* the personality or traits of the people in your life. As I have said before—but it bears repeating because so many people forget it when push comes to shove—*do not try to directly change a manipulator!*

Instead, focus your efforts on *you*—on your *choices* and on the *control* you exercise and must preserve over your own behavior, thoughts, and feelings. If you comply with the influence efforts of a manipulator—that is, if you give him what he wants—you will reward and encourage the manipulation to continue. If, however, you correctly identify the manipulative dynamic, you can *choose* to respond differently—to make the manipulation ineffective by ceasing to let it work.

The Usual Suspects

What kind of people, then, might be pulling your strings? Who are the usual suspects?

The answer lies in identifying the characteristic personality traits, needs, and behaviors of people who are most likely to manipulate others to serve their own purposes. The categories or personality types that follow should not be viewed as mutually exclusive. In other words, people can and do fall into more than one category. Also, this is not an exhaustive list of everyone who manipulates. It is an attempt to characterize the personality types that are most likely to use manipulation in their relationships.

Please note also that several of the descriptions that follow are of discrete, defined, diagnosable personality *disorders*. While some people may not evidence the full array of traits and behaviors necessary to meet the criteria of diagnosis as defined by the American Psychiatric Association's *Diagnostic and Statistical Manual of Mental Disorders* (DSM-IV)—the "bible" of mental health professionals—they may display several of the traits that comprise a disorder. If you recognize a pattern of traits from the categories below (not just one or two in isolation) in one or more of the people in your life with whom you may be having difficulty, you should be sensitized to the very real possibility that manipulation may be present.

And as you read through the following list, see if I am describing anyone you know.

The Machiavellian Personality

In the early 1970s, psychologist Richard Christie and his colleagues identified a distinct personality style that is characterized by manipulativeness, cynicism about human nature, and shrewdness in interpersonal behavior. Named after the sixteenth-century political philosopher and Italian Prince Machiavelli, this personality style is very nearly synonymous with being a manipulator. Machiavellian personalities are committed to the proposition that a desired end justifies virtually any means. *Machiavellianism* is defined as a manipulative strategy of social interaction and personality style that uses other people as tools of personal gain.

Christie developed a test that measures the tendency to be machiavellian. People who score high on this measure are referred to as "high machs." High machs select situations that are loosely structured and unencumbered by rules that restrict the deployment of exploitative strategies. They tend to evoke specific reactions from others, such as anger and retaliation for having been exploited. High machs influence or manipulate others in predictable ways, using tactics that are exploitative, self-serving, and nearly always deceptive.

Machiavellianism derives from the views of Prince Machiavelli that a ruler is not bound by traditional ethical norms.

A prince, therefore, should only be concerned with power and be bound only by rules that would lead to success. Prince Machiavelli deduced these rules from the political practices of his time:

- Never show humility; it is more effective to show arrogance when dealing with others.
- Morality and ethics are for the weak; powerful people should feel free to lie, cheat, and deceive whenever it suits their purpose.
- It is better to be feared than loved.

In contemporary terms, high machs tend to endorse the following statements:

1. The best way to handle people is to tell them what they want to hear.
2. Anyone who completely trusts anyone else is asking for trouble.
3. It is safest to assume that all people have a vicious streak and that it will come out when they are given a chance.
4. Most people will work hard only when they are forced to do so.
5. It is hard to get ahead without cutting corners and bending the rules.

And high machs tend to *disagree* with the following statements:

1. When you ask someone to do something for you, it is best to give the real reason for wanting it rather than giving reasons that might carry more weight.

2. It is never right to lie to someone else.
3. Most people are basically good and kind.
4. One should take action only when it is morally right.

High machs tend to constitute a distinctive type. They tend to be charming, confident, and glib; but they also are arrogant, calculating, and cynical, prone to manipulate and exploit. In the context of laboratory experiment games, high machs display a keen and opportunistic sense of timing, and they appear to capitalize especially in situations that contain ambiguity regarding the rules.

Narcissistic Personality Disorder

A second personality type that is very likely to engage in manipulation of others is the narcissistic personality type. People with *narcissistic personality disorder* have the mixed blessing of holding an extremely inflated self-image and a strong sense of entitlement that makes them insensitive to the needs and feelings of other people.

According to DSM-IV, people with this disorder have a pattern of grandiosity, a need to be admired, and a lack of empathy for others' feelings or needs. A narcissistic personality is expressed by having *at least five* of the following maladaptive traits:

1. An overinflated sense of one's own importance and an exaggerated sense of one's achievements and talents
2. The tendency to spend hours fantasizing about having unlimited success, power, brilliance, beauty, and the "perfect" romance
3. The belief that one is so special and unique that one should only associate with other special or high-status people and institutions

4. The requirement of excessive admiration from others
5. The belief that one is entitled to special treatment or that others should automatically comply with one's expectations
6. The desire to exploit others to get what one needs for oneself
7. The inability to recognize or empathize with the feelings and needs of others
8. Constant envy of other people's achievements or possessions
9. Arrogance and haughtiness

The one quality among all others that narcissists have that makes them most likely to manipulate others is their strong sense of *entitlement*. This means that the narcissist simply *expects* special favors or accommodations from others without assuming reciprocal responsibilities in turn. As a result, if or when the mark does not comply or do what is wanted, the narcissist will express anger or surprise.

Feeling entitled allows the narcissist to use others almost automatically for his own personal gain. In fact, the only people who matter to the narcissist are those who will in some way further his ends, advance his position, or enhance his self-image. The narcissist simply expects that others *must* cater to him and defer to his needs and priorities. The exploitation takes place in the context of a near-thorough disregard for the personal integrity and rights of others. For example, narcissistic employers or managers tend to drive their employees beyond their endurance with complete disregard for the toll their demands take on the personal lives of their emlpoyees.

The narcissist displays a clear lack of empathy for others. He is quite simply unable (and/or unwilling) to recognize how others feel. For example, if a friend falls ill, the manipulator may express irritation with the ways in which the friend's illness is inconveniencing him (e.g., the friend stays home in bed rather than accompanying the manipulator to a party or other event) without any recognition or appreciation of the distress felt by the sick friend.

Narcissists' relationships are predictably one-sided and problematic. Others view narcissists as arrogant, selfish, demanding, cold, and aloof.

Borderline Personality Disorder

The term *borderline* is somewhat misleading. It does not mean bordering on the edge of mental illness. Rather, *borderline personality disorder* refers to a pattern of personality that involves highly unstable relationships, a constantly changing self-image, mood fluctuations, and difficulty controlling impulses.

For the borderline, life is extremely intense and chaotic or tumultuous. While there are certainly some wonderful experiences, these are invariably punctuated by terrible moments caused by rapid and dramatic shifts in the way the borderline feels about herself and about other people.

As a result, for example, the borderline may think of her lover or partner as the most wonderful person she has ever met. But this attitude can shift drastically to one of devaluation and even contempt triggered by a disappointment that somehow proves to the borderline that the partner does not care enough about her or understand what she needs. This sudden precipitous shift catches the mark off balance and makes him vulnerable to manipulation.

Borderlines are characteristically terrified of being abandoned, and they will go to great lengths to avoid separations.

They become hypersensitive to any sign of rejection. Borderlines will lash out in eruptive anger when their security feels threatened. They may display emotional tantrums, usually when faced with rejection or the threat of abandonment, or simply show disappointment, but they often feel guilty and ashamed following their loss of emotional control.

According to the DSM-IV, borderline personality disorder is a pattern expressed by an individual having *at least five* of the following maladaptive traits:

1. Making frantic efforts to avoid real or imagined abandonment
2. Having relationships with others that are intense and have lots of ups and downs
3. A constantly shifting sense of self-identity (e.g., who one is and what one believes in)
4. Difficulty keeping self-destructive impulses under control
5. Suicide threats or attempts or attempts to mutilate one's body (e.g., cutting or burning arms or other areas of the body)
6. Rapidly shifting moods alternating between intense sadness, irritability, and anxiety
7. A feeling deep down inside that there is just emptiness
8. Anger that is often well out of proportion to the circumstances
9. Feelings of paranoia or detachment when under a lot of stress (i.e., feeling as though in a dream)

People with borderline personality disorder manipulate others primarily through evocation of negative emotional responses. Those who are involved with borderlines learn rather quickly that chronic uncertainty, anxiety, frustration, and hostility become the characteristic reactions to the borderline's disruptive and unstable behavior.

Those involved in relationships with borderlines often feel controlled or taken advantage of through means such as threats, no-win situations, the silent treatment, rages, and other methods that the borderline's partner or mark view as unfair.

Borderlines are prone to use a highly manipulative method labeled as "emotional blackmail" by Susan Forward (1997) in a book of the same name. *Emotional blackmail* is defined as a direct or indirect threat by someone to punish others if they do not do what the blackmailer wants. The basic threat of emotional blackmail is straightforward: If you do not behave as I want you to, I will make you suffer. Young children who throw temper tantrums have perfected the drill, although they are typically too young to be classified as borderlines. Nevertheless, the same principle applies.

Being involved with a borderline is tantamount to being strapped into an emotional roller coaster bound for endless cycles of drama and chaos, *Sturm und Drang*. The partner is typically subjected to every shift in the borderline's mood, which may change from normal to depressed, cheerful to irritable, and seemingly calm to raging angry and anxious all on a moment's notice and often in ways that the partner cannot anticipate or even understand.

Over time, the partner experiences continual frustration as a result of the borderline's erratic moods and insatiable demands for reassurance. Eventually, the frustration of the partner may build to anger and even to the rejection that the borderline most fears but helps to create.

Feeling manipulated is a nearly universal reaction of those involved with borderlines. From the vantage point of the borderline, he may be acting impulsively out of fear, loneliness, desperation, and even hopelessness rather than out of malicious or cruel intention. Nevertheless, while borderlines may not *intend* to manipulate or engage in devious and intentional acts aimed at controlling or influencing the behavior of others, the net result and the highly negative impact on others with whom they are closely involved remain the same.

Dependent Personality Disorder

People with a *dependent personality disorder* have an excessive need to be taken care of, which leads to their being overly submissive and clinging. Dependent personalities are needy, submissive, helpless, and incapable of functioning unless they receive constant nurturance, approval, reassurance, and emotional support. Because they have trouble making their own decisions on subjects large or small, others involved with dependent personalities get manipulated into assuming responsibility for making or aiding in all their decisions. In effect, others assume control and responsibility over the lives of their dependent partners.

Because dependent personalities rely so much on others, they fail to learn age-appropriate decision-making skills. In turn, this perpetuates and reinforces their feelings of inadequacy, childishness, and dependency. To reduce expectations of others, the dependent personality frequently will fake ineptitude, constantly trying to get others to do what he or she could do himself or herself.

Dependent people become very anxious when left alone because they are so reliant on others. They need others to tell them who to be with, where to live, what type of job (if any) to seek, what clothes to wear, where and what to eat, where to go on vacation, how to spend money, and even how to raise their own children.

Criticism is taken at face value because it confirms their negative self-image. Because they find the idea of losing the guidance of others downright terrifying, dependent personalities will not express disagreement or dissent even if they do disagree with advice given. Furthermore, they will not express any anger even when provoked because their need to be taken care of is paramount, and they cannot risk rejection or separation from the people they manipulate into taking care of them.

According to the DSM-IV, a person has dependent personality disorder if he has an excessive need to be taken care of, which leads to being overly submissive and clinging. The pattern is expressed by an individual having *at least five* of the following maladaptive traits:

1. An inability to make everyday decisions without advice and reassurance from others
2. Reliance on others to take responsibility for most of the major areas in one's life
3. Difficulty disagreeing with those whose support or approval is needed
4. Difficulty getting started on new projects or tasks or doing things on one's own without help from others
5. Going to such great lengths to obtain nurturance and support from others that one ends up volunteering to do things that are unpleasant or that really puts one out
6. Feelings of discomfort or helplessness when alone based on a belief that one is unable to take care of oneself

7. Desperately seeking out a new relationship immediately after a close relationship ends so to replace it (i.e., a rebound relationship)
8. Excessive worry about what will happen if there is no one to take care of oneself

The manipulation of a dependent personality is obvious, although—as with the borderline—it is not necessarily conscious, intentional, or planned. By virtue of the helplessness, submissiveness, neediness, and abdication of responsibility for their own lives, dependent personalities manipulate others to take care of them and to make their life decisions for them.

There is often a gender difference with respect to how the dependency in this personality type is presented. Women tend to be submissive as a way of manipulating or getting others to take care of them; men, on the other hand, are more often demanding and pushy toward those they need. Despite the overt pushiness and demanding style, however, these men may be every bit as dependent as the more obviously submissive women.

Histrionic Personality Disorder

The word *histrionic* means "dramatic or theatrical." People with this disorder attempt to get attention in strange and unusual ways. The basic characteristic of these individuals is a pattern of attention seeking and being excessively emotional, if not downright melodramatic.

The histrionic's excessive emotionality frequently manifests as rapid shifts in emotion that come across as superficial or artificial. Such a person may overreact emotionally or sexually to situations.

Histrionic individuals have an intense craving for attention, and they feel uncomfortable when they are not the center of attention. They often dress flamboyantly or wear outrageous hairstyles to gain attention. They frequently act in a very sexual or seductive manner in their continual attempt to win people's attention and affection. Because they must be the constant center of attention, histrionic personalities can become very manipulative, frequently using emotional explosions to get their way.

Histrionic personalities are highly impressionable. As such, they are often overly trusting and gullible. They tend to follow the latest trends in fashion, music, and so on, even when their interest is not age-appropriate (i.e., they work hard to look younger than they really are).

Histrionic personalities are usually vain and self-absorbed. They tend to have only superficial relationships, and their emotional expressions and speech often seem not to be genuine or to lack a depth of feeling.

According to the DSM-IV, a person has histrionic personality disorder if there is a pattern of seeking attention and displaying emotions excessively. The pattern is expressed by having *at least five* of the following maladaptive traits:

1. Feelings of discomfort when one is in situations in which one is not the center of attention
2. Frequently acting in a sexually seductive or provocative way that is inappropriate to the situation
3. Showing emotions that appear to others to be rapidly shifting, shallow, and superficial
4. Consistently using physical appearance to draw attention to oneself
5. Talking in an excessively impressionistic way that is lacking in specific detail

6. Tending to be overly dramatic and theatrical when expressing oneself or in telling a story
7. Being overly suggestible and easily influenced by others' opinions
8. Tending to view relationships as more intimate than they really are

Histrionic personalities often play both roles—that of the manipulator and that of the person being manipulated. Like the borderline and dependent personalities described earlier, the histrionic personality manipulates largely out of evocation—she evokes negative reactions in others in response to the expression of characteristic traits.

Her seductive and sexual behavior—which is meant to be more social than explicitly sexual to the histrionic—can easily manipulate others into responding sexually. In turn, this can lead to embarrassment and to more serious concerns or issues of sexual harassment. Histrionics frequently are raped—or cry rape. Or after a sexual encounter, they threaten to cry rape.

The most intrusive form of manipulation of histrionics derives from their need to be the center of attention. In a group setting, for example, a histrionic will try to upstage whoever else is talking or gaining the attention of the group. Or through excessive emotionality (crying, explosive outbursts, and so on), the histrionic will manipulate others into paying attention even if they do not wish to do so.

Passive-Aggressive Personalities

Although passive-aggressive personality no longer appears in the DSM-IV as a diagnosable disorder, individuals who display the traits of this personality type can be highly manipulative. The key to understanding passive-aggressive individuals is to recognize that they display their own hostility or aggression through passive rather than overt, actively aggressive means. However, through their passive resistance to the demands or needs of others, they often elicit extreme frustration and eventually evoke overt hostility in others.

The most common maneuvers of a passive-aggressive personality are procrastination, dawdling, stubbornness, intentional inefficiency, and forgetfulness. Typically, passive-aggressive personalities complain to others about the demands that higher-ups make of them. For example, if the boss requests a project, the passive-aggressive personality will not resist directly. Instead, he or she will whine, sulk, and complain to coworkers or family about the excessive and "unreasonable" demands that have been placed on him or her.

The modus operandi for resisting is to "forget" a deadline, miss meetings, and delay and procrastinate until those who are depending on him or her become frustrated and even enraged.

In personal relationships, the passive-aggressive personality resists demands through passive means. For example, if asked to a social occasion, the passive-aggressive person may comply or go along with the request but display his resistance through becoming quiet, withdrawn, and sullen at the occasion itself. When the partner becomes upset with his uncommunicative behavior, the passive-aggressive person will express surprise and confusion over the partner's reaction.

In a word, passive-aggressive personalities manipulate others through their very passivity. By *not* doing what is required of them or by *seemingly* complying with requests that are then sabotaged through passive resistance, the passive-aggressive personality manipulates others by evoking frustration and hostility. They are unlikely to change and display very poor insight or understanding of how their passive resistance affects others.

Ultimately, of course, the passive-aggressive personality will manipulate others into making fewer and fewer demands of him because the emotional cost of relying on such an individual is too great.

Type A Angry Personalities

Type A is a designation given to a high-stress personality and behavior pattern. In the mid-1970s when the original Type A research was done (exclusively on men), the researchers correlated the presence of Type A traits in males with a much greater risk of cardiovascular disease than was true of their counterparts who did not exhibit Type A traits.

The essence of the Type A personality is someone with "hurry sickness." Such individuals are concerned with getting more and more done in less and less time. In today's parlance, they are typically multitaskers who become stressed and angry if they are caught in a traffic snarl, if they have to wait in line, or even if they have to wait for others to finish a sentence or thought.

In addition to the self-induced pressure of hurry sickness, Type A's are characterized as highly competitive, concerned with quantitative measures of success (how much money one is earning, how many promotions one has garnered, how many possessions one has) as opposed to the qualitative measures of life (how happy or healthy one is, how satisfied or fulfilled one might be). Type A personalities are also very concerned with maintaining control over their environments, including the people in them.

Over many years of research on the high-stress personality dubbed Type A, it has been shown that the true core trait that makes these personality types prone to cardiac and other illnesses is the free-floating anger and hostility they display. For Type A's, hostility is on a perpetual hair trigger. Their hyper style places them and those around them in a state of continual pressure. Consequently, anything that foils their plans, backs up their schedule, or otherwise frustrates their desire to maintain control results in an expression of anger. And it is the anger and hostility they harbor that become toxic to them and that translate physically into coronary artery disease.

Naturally, Type A intensity, stress, competitiveness, and anger are not limited just to men, although most of the research has been done on male samples. Some years ago, aware that the Type A research had been done exclusively on males, I wrote a book called *The Type E Woman: How to Overcome the Stress of Being Everything to Everybody*. My thesis was—and remains—that many women who fill multiples roles (e.g., career, mother, chauffer, cook, housekeeper, volunteer, daughter/sister/friend, and on and on) tend to have as much or even more stress in their lives than most Type A men, but the stress is different and requires different treatment and solutions.

Nevertheless, Type A personalities are controlling, angry, and often intimidating. They manipulate others directly by explicit tactics of control. However, they also manipulate others indirectly by evoking avoidance strategies in others who do not wish to be the target of their hostility.

Consequently, people who work for or with these angry Type A personalities or who are involved with them personally often feel that they must "walk on eggshells" to avoid upsetting them. If those who are involved with angry Type A's are conflict-avoidant and fearful of confrontations, they are likely to become highly controlled and intimidated by the mere threat of an outburst or confrontation.

Angry, controlling personalities can manipulate those around them in other ways as well. The phenomenon of *stress contagion* is quite palpable around such individuals. In other words, their stress level causes everyone around them to feel stressed and anxious as well.

The Con or Antisocial Personality Disorder

People with this disorder have a lifelong pattern of irresponsible behavior and show little concern for the rights of others, the norms of society, the dictates of conscience, or the law. There is a marked gender difference, with far more men being diagnosed with this disorder than women.

Antisocial personalities begin young. As youngsters, they typically lie when it suits them and steal if they think they can get away with it. In adulthood, they move on to bigger and better "cons." Antisocial personalities tend to have tumultuous lives with sudden changes in relationships, jobs, and residences. They may engage in illegal activities, including fraud, theft, white-collar crime, or drug dealing. They display very poor frustration tolerance and easily get irritated and even aggressive if things do not go their way.

These personalities tend to be reckless and blasé about their own safety and that of others. They will take extreme chances with unsafe sex, excessive speeding, heavy alcohol and substance abuse, and even dangerous criminal activities.

Antisocial personalities are self-serving and arrogant. Often slick, smooth talkers, they believe that individuals should and do look out for themselves only. Their decisions generally are impulsive, irresponsible, and spontaneous, lacking any consideration for the consequences of their acts. They are irresponsible in financial matters, write bad checks, default on debts, and are callously indifferent to the effects these actions may have on others.

Charm and charisma are used skillfully to deceive, manipulate, and con others. They lie with impunity, think nothing of using aliases, and seek to con others for profit or just for sport or fun. Since they believe that others are out to attack and exploit them, they feel quite justified in striking first or preemptively to get others before others get them. These personalities are adept at using glib rationalizations to justify their behavior, frequently blaming their victims for being stupid, gullible, or helpless and claiming that they had it coming to them. They endorse the belief that if they did not take advantage of their victims, someone else would.

Antisocial personalities fail to develop a conscience. As such, they experience little or no guilt or remorse for hurting others or for the suffering they inflict on others. Antisocial personalities are among the most manipulative and dangerous people you may ever have the bad fortune to meet or, worse, become involved with or fall prey to. Avoid them at all costs.

Addictive Personalities

Since addiction, by definition, makes its object (e.g., alcohol, drugs, gambling) the number one priority, other people in an addict's life necessarily take a backseat. While addiction-prone personalities are not included in the DSM-IV list of personality disorders, they certainly and indisputably cause a great deal of suffering—both physical and psychological—for those with whom they are involved. Spend one evening at an Al-Anon meeting with the spouses, children, and other codependents (i.e., those who are dependent on the person who is addicted), and you will get an instant picture of the damage that addiction causes.

Addicts notoriously lie, deny, exploit others, and wreak havoc with their families, work, and social relationships. Alcoholics and addicts manipulate others by their habits and by the pattern of maladaptive personality traits and interpersonal behaviors that support their addiction.

Those who are close to addicts try nearly everything to get them to stop drinking or using and to become clean and sober. However, as the addiction increases and the quality of the alcoholic's or addict's life spirals downward, his habit manipulates others into feelings of guilt, depression, humiliation, anger, frustration, uncertainty, low self-esteem, and other toxic emotions that the addict and his addiction create.

The addict's extreme neediness—which becomes greater as his addiction worsens and his debilitation increases—fits the often excessive, complementary needs of the codependent to take care of others at the expense of her own health and well-being. Thus the addict's problems become highly detrimental not only to himself but also to the codependent personalities with whom he is linked.

Until an alcoholic or addict decides to change his behavior, nothing anyone else does will make a difference.

An Exercise in Spotting Manipulators

Go back and take another look at the five case studies in Chapter 2. See if you can identify discrete personality types or styles among the characters described. Then take a look around your own life. Can you spot possible manipulators?

How Do Your Strings Get Pulled?

In this chapter you have read and learned about the most likely manipulators in your midst. These personality types are known to use manipulation as a regular, preferred, and often effective method in their interpersonal relationships.

As you read over these personality descriptions, you may have recognized some of the people in your life with whom you have had or currently have difficulty. Recognizing these personality traits and patterns will sensitize you to the possibility that manipulation is taking place.

Just how do these manipulators operate? What are the methods they use, and what tactics do they use? This is the subject of Chapter 7.

7

How Manipulation Works

HAVE YOU EVER BEEN BAFFLED by a magic trick? Have you ever been mystified watching a person being sawed in half? Did you ever watch a skilled prestidigitator conjure a rabbit out of his hat and say, "How did he do that? How does that work?"

When my daughter was about 3 years old, my husband taught her a parlor trick called "Black Magic." Here's how it worked: She would exit a room full of people, and someone would then point to any object or even a person in the room. Let's say a bowl was picked. When my husband called my daughter back into the room, he would ask her, "Is it the couch? Is it the chair? Is it the rug? Is it the picture?" and she would correctly answer "No" to each question until she was asked about the bowl, and she would confidently say, "Yes."

The object of the game was for people to guess how the trick was accomplished—and almost no one ever guessed! No matter how many times the trick was performed, my daughter always selected correctly. And people—children and adults—would ask tons of questions ("Is it your voice inflection? Are you secretly pointing to the object? Is it always the fourth object you pick?")

all to no avail. They were stymied. After a while, some adults started to get frustrated because a young child was stumping them.

Now while it would not be right for me to spoil the trick by telling you how it is done, I can tell you that it is very simple. It had to be; my daughter could do it when she was only three. (She also could do the part my husband played; he would leave the room, and then she would ask him the questions when he returned.) To me, it is also very obvious. But, over the years, as I watched the two of them do the trick many times, I always marveled that people were missing the most obvious clues. However, when you know how something works, it is always easy to spot the trick when someone else does it.

Manipulation, simply stated, is much like a magic trick. If you take the time to learn how manipulation works, it is less likely that you will be caught off guard when confronted with it because you will know what to look for. The mystery will be gone.

How Do You Get Manipulated?

Manipulative relationships depend on activating one (or both) of two principal human drives: gain (or reward) and loss (or avoidance). These are the two engines that drive the manipulation. Do not bother looking for anything more complicated than this: Manipulation always boils down to the promise of a net gain and/or the threat of a net loss.

In some manipulative relationships, there is the promise of something valuable to gain, which is why the mark willingly goes along with the program. Or the manipulator promises to reward the cooperative mark—or compliant victim—with something that he or she wants, needs, desires, or prefers.

A typical work situation might have a superior asking a subordinate to do something distasteful—maybe work late or come in on Saturday. It is implied or even stated overtly that this is how people get ahead in this company, by going the extra mile. The mark might be told, "If you expect to get that promotion [or that raise], you'll be here on Saturday. Of course, the choice is always yours," the boss adds. Some choice.

This is fairly blatant, but sometimes the action is much more subtle, and it is harder to see or feel the manipulation. The point is that in this case the manipulation promises to reward the compliant victim with something or someone she desires, needs, or prefers.

It is also important to understand that in many situations just like this the mark does not always know that she is being manipulated. Sometimes it feels more like influence or a suggestion. However, when the other side of the coin is examined—meaning the consequences if the mark does not go along with the "request" or "suggestion"—it ceases to be influence and is downright manipulative behavior.

This happens when there is something valuable to lose or something one wants to avoid. A skilled manipulator then plays on the victim's fears and promises to prevent the loss or perhaps to avoid the punishing consequence if the requested compliance or cooperation is demonstrated.

Control Levers

The drivers cannot drive themselves, however. They require certain essential levers of control to make them operate.

All manipulative relationships depend on certain levers of control that are used to hold out the promise of *gain* or the fear of *loss* or the means to *avoid* something that is undesirable. For example, common levers of *gain* or *reward* include

- Money
- Power
- Status (e.g., titles, promotions, admission to a school or club)
- Sex
- Approval
- Love
- Acceptance
- Commitment (such as to a relationship)
- Praise
- Reassurance
- Material gifts
- Companionship

It is perhaps easier now to look at this list and recall a time when someone used one of these levers of control on you. If you were in a position where you craved money or power or a promotion or entrance into an exclusive club, and someone came along and dangled the brass ring in front of you, you may have leaped at it without being aware that you were being manipulated. This is so because what someone was offering was something you wanted, and you viewed what he or she was saying as influence as opposed to outright manipulation.

When a promise of gain is the lever of control, the manipulation can seem soft or subtle. Hard, direct manipulation, however, is just the opposite side of the same coin. Look at the following list of some common levers of *loss, avoidance,* or *fear*:

- Loss of money
- Loss of power
- Loss of status

- Loss of job
- Loss of opportunity for advancement
- Loss of any of the other rewards
- Loss of the opportunity to gain such rewards

When a manipulator suddenly shifts levers from promise of gain to threat of loss, you will know it. And you will know that you are being manipulated. It is like being outside and enjoying the sun on a beautiful fall day. Suddenly, a dark cloud blocks the sun, and the air turns decidedly colder, forcing you to pull your collar up around your neck. The chill you feel is the same sensation you should feel when promise of gain crosses over to threat of loss. The manipulation suddenly becomes coercive and stressful.

Keep in mind that manipulation often turns on the presentation or promise of rewards *followed by* the more insidious stage in which the threat of loss of the desired reward is issued. In other words, if someone offers you a gain, and either that gain or the promise of that gain does not satisfy the manipulator's motives, you may next be confronted with the loss of that gain or the loss of something else in order to make the manipulation succeed.

However, there are more levers of control when loss, avoidance, and/or fear are threatened:

- Fear of conflict
- Fear of anger
- Fear of rejection or abandonment
- Fear of conditional love being withdrawn
- Fear of failure
- Fear of exposure (e.g., of secrets, flaws, inadequacies)
- Fear of shame
- Fear of guilt

- Fear of criticism
- Fear of the loss of communication (i.e., the silent treatment; withdrawal of willingness to talk about the problem)
- Fear of withholding of affection or sex

Take a moment to reread the lists of control levers. When you become familiar with them, your antennae will be raised so that you will be more alert and able to see manipulation coming. Later I will talk about what to do when you are being manipulated, but for now it is important that you are in a position to recognize manipulation when it is on you. In baseball terms, raising your awareness is like learning to spot a curve ball as soon as it leaves the pitcher's glove. Even skilled baseball players can hit a curve ball only every once in a while. But just think how much higher their averages would be if the catcher whispered in their ear, "The next pitch will be a curve."

This is what these lists are designed to help you do: recognize the manipulative curved pitch. Shortly I will be looking over your swing.

What Does the Manipulator Want?

In simple terms, the manipulator wants one of two things from you:

- He wants you to *do* something.
- He wants you to *stop doing* something.

In psychological terms, the manipulator is trying to either:

- *Instigate* behavior from you. In other words, he is trying to get you to do something that is in his self-interest but may or may not be in your own. Remember, the manipulator always puts *his* self-interest above yours. *Always.*

- Or *stop you* from doing something. She is seeking to *terminate* some behavior that you are currently doing but that she wants you to stop.

As you can see—and will continue to see—manipulators are often devious but not always very deep. This means that once you know that you are in a manipulative situation (recognizing the pitch as its delivered), you will be in a stronger position to see the manipulation as it takes place.

The gain or loss that compliance (with either the instigation or the termination) promises may be made explicit by the manipulator (e.g., promise of gratitude or approval, promise of a tangible reward, and so on), or it may remain implicit or unverbalized (e.g., loss of approval or disapproval, loss of opportunity for that hoped-for promotion or some other reward, or fear of these things happening).

What Types of Relationships Are Susceptible to Manipulation?

As I noted earlier, manipulation can occur in every type of relationship. Manipulation is defined by the setup of the promised gain or the promise to avoid loss and by the tactics used and the conditional outcomes that are perceived. Therefore, any relationship that has the potential to have an impact on your identity, security, status, self-worth, and sense of personal adequacy has the highest manipulative potential because you have the most to gain or the most to lose from the outcome.

For these reasons, manipulation frequently occurs in:

- Family relationships, including marriage and children and other relatives
- Sexual/romantic relationships (including ex-spouses)

- Work relationships, either peer or nonpeer
- Friendships
- Academic relationships (teacher/student)
- Professional relationships (e.g., doctor/patient; lawyer/client)

What Tactics Does the Manipulator Use?

Manipulators tend to use multiple tactics to gain your compliance with their instigation or termination desires, but usually not simultaneously. This would be too obvious. Typically, they will try one tactic, and if that fails, they will up the ante.

The tactics used will vary depending on the nature of the relationship between you and the manipulator. For example, the tactics used by your spouse or romantic partner likely will differ from those used by your boss or supervisor at work. Similarly, the tactics used by family members likely also will differ from those used by a friend or coworker.

One study conducted by David Buss and his colleagues (Buss et al., 1987)* identified the tactics used by dating couples in their attempts to manipulate one another's behavior. These researchers identified six primary tactics of manipulation used for both attempts to instigate and attempts to terminate behaviors in their respective partners.

(It is important to note that the couples studied did not represent a clinical sample where manipulation had become a problem. Instead, these researchers attempted to understand the principal ways in which couples acknowledged trying to influence and/or manipulate one another's behavior. The

---

*Buss, D.M., Gomes, M., Higgins, D.S., and Lauterbach, K. "Tactics of manipulation," *Journal of Personality and Social Psychology*, Vol. 52, No. 6 (1987), 1219–1279.

results are interesting and useful for our purposes because they capture six important tactics that are used commonly in many different types of relationships.)

Recognizing the six tactics discussed below as types of manipulation will again help sensitize you to manipulative attempts made by people in your life. How many of the following have you used, and how many have been used on you by others?

The first tactic identified is the use of *charm*. Examples of this charm tactic include:

- I compliment her so that she will do it (or stop it).
- I act charming so that he will do it (or stop it).
- I try to be loving and romantic when I ask her.
- I give him a small gift or card before I ask.
- I tell her that I will do her a favor if she will do it (or stop it).

The second tactic used by couples to manipulate their partner is the *silent treatment*. Examples include:

- I do not respond to him until he does it (or stops it).
- I ignore her until she does it (or stops it).
- I am silent until he agrees to do it (or stop it).
- I refuse to do something she likes until she does it (or stops it).

The third tactic is *coercion*. Examples include:

- I demand that she do it (or stop it).
- I yell at him until he does it (or stops it).
- I criticize her for not doing it (or stopping it).
- I curse at her until she does it (or stops it).
- I threaten him with something if he does not do it (or stops it).

The fourth tactic is *reason*. Examples include:

- I give her reasons for why she should do it (or stop it).
- I ask him why he does not do it (or stop it).
- I point out all the good things that will come from doing it (or stopping it).
- I explain why I want her to do it (or stop it).
- I show him that I would be willing to do it for him.

The fifth tactic is *regression*. Examples include:

- I pout until she does it (or stops it).
- I sulk until she does it (or stops it).

And the sixth and final tactic identified by Buss and his colleagues is *debasement*. Examples include:

- I allow myself to be debased so she will do it (or stop it).
- I lower myself so that he will do it (or stop it).
- I act humble so she will do it (or stop it.)

These six tactics of manipulation are not limited just to dating couples. In fact, you are likely to encounter some or all of them in many of your relationships. However, there are some additional tactics that are used commonly in certain relationships that would not likely be used by couples. For example, in work relationships, where there is a clear line of authority (from your boss or supervisor to you; from you to a subordinate), the manipulation may occur using *authority* as a tactic. An example is being told directly or ordered/directed to do something (or stop).

In family relationships, *guilt induction* is a common tactic. This might fall under the general category of *coercion* but warrants mention here because so many people are particularly sensitive to the use of guilt in family manipulation. Guilt can be induced with just a calculated tone of voice that can turn what might otherwise be a straightforward request into a shower of guilt. A mother who says, "Gee, we were all hoping that you'd be able to come home for the holidays instead of going off with your friends," can heap a wallop of guilt on the statement with just the right tonal inflection.

Tactics are often stacked up in a holding pattern like planes waiting to land at a busy airport. For example, if charm fails, the silent treatment or coercion may be used. Similarly, if reason fails, charm may be used, followed by regression. However, it is rare that tactics are tried in combination because they could collide with each other.

Think about the people in your life, and try to categorize the ways or tactics they use to get you to do something or to stop doing something.

When Are You Most Susceptible to Manipulation?

Manipulative relationships can occur at any time in your life, but you are most vulnerable when:

- *You are in a transition*—moving from one developmental stage to another (from childhood to adolescence, from adolescence to adulthood)
- *You are making a significant life change*—positive or negative—such as marriage, parenthood, promotion, or job loss
- You are thinking about setting a life change in motion (e.g., contemplating divorce)

- You have suffered a substantial loss
- You are in a period of heightened instability and uncertainty

These periods involve redefinition of identity, greater stress and anxiety, and a greater sense of vulnerability/opportunity for *gain* and *loss*. For these reasons, the magnitude and impact of desired gains and losses are intensified greatly.

What this means is that you should be particularly on your guard against manipulators during these vulnerable periods. Truly skilled manipulators are like vultures—they can sense when a prey is weak. For example, in a first or new job, your need for *gains* or *rewards* in the form of promotions, approval from your supervisors, and acceptance by your coworkers—coupled with your inexperience—may make you a likely mark for a manipulative coworker or boss.

Francine, in Chapter 2, is such a target for the manipulative senior broker, Arnie. Or a man who is newly single or a woman who feels her "biological clock" ticking loudly may be very desirous of a relationship that will lead to marriage. Because of the intensity of the need, the possibility of being manipulated by someone who holds out the promise of commitment may be great.

In Chapter 8 you will have an opportunity to examine your current need system. As you will soon see, the areas where you feel most in need of *gains* and/or most fearful or concerned about *losses* are actually the hooks by which you are most likely to be reeled into a manipulative relationship.

8

What Are Your Hooks?

THIS CHAPTER is really for you to write rather than just to read. I want you to take an inventory of your needs at this point in your life. According to the mechanics of manipulation, a manipulator will sink his or her hooks into the areas of your personality where you have the strongest desired *gains*—what you really want or need most at this point in your life—and/or where you have the strongest or greatest *fears of loss*. Skilled manipulators seem to have a sixth sense about sniffing out where they can take advantage of your *desired gains* or *fears of loss*. Sometimes, however, you may just make it easy for them.

For example, you may be quite open and expressive to certain people in your life about your aspirations, needs, desires, and dreams, and you might be quite open about your fears of loss. On the other hand, you may not talk openly to many people, if anyone, about these deep desires or worries. In fact, you may be entirely unaware that your needs show at all.

Being candid with yourself and understanding your own need system is a basic and important step in making yourself a harder and more resistant target to manipulators. Remember, manipulators use certain levers of control over their targets that hold the *promise of gain*, stimulate the *fear of loss*, or offer the *means to avoid* something that is highly undesirable to the mark.

Therefore, take out a pad of paper, and get ready to look carefully and candidly at yourself. There are only two questions I want to ask you, although you may have multiple answers.

Question 1: What Do You Most Want or Need at This Point in Your Life?

Think about the areas of potential gain listed below. Consider each, and give each a rating from 1 to 5 where

    1 = no need at all
    2 = low need
    3 = moderately strong need
    4 = strong need
    5 = very strong to strongest need

Now rate the following 1 to 5 according to your needs:

— Money
— Power
— Position/status
    ✔ Security
    ✔ Love
    ✔ Sexual fulfillment
    ✔ Approval

Acceptance
Commitment
Family
Spouse
Children
Life partner
Long-term relationship
Happiness
Freedom from worry
Job/career attainments
Praise
Reassurance *(that I shouldn't feel guilty abt my good life)*
Material possessions/gifts
Friends/companionship
Success/achievement
Good physical health
Good emotional health
Relaxation
Laughter
Self-esteem
Freedom
Education
Competence
Other (specify): *Commitment (satisfying) to something other than myself*

For each of the gains you rated as a 3 or higher, write a short paragraph or two expanding on the concept and making it personally applicable to you and your life. For example, whose love or approval do you need? What kind of security do you desire?

The goal is for you to tell yourself in as much detail as possible what your areas of need or potential gain are.

Question 2: What Do You Worry About or Fear the Most About Losing?

Read each item on the list below, and rate each on a 1 to 5 point scale where

    1 = not worried at all
    2 = low degree of worry or fear
    3 = moderate degree of worry or fear
    4 = strong degree of worry or fear
    5 = very strong to strongest degree of worry and fear.

Next, rate the following 1 to 5 according to your fears:

    Loss of money
    Demotion of power, position, or status
    Loss of job/career
    Loss of opportunity for gain as above
    Loss of love
    Loss of sex/sexual fulfillment
    Fear of conflict or confrontation
    Fear of rejection
    Fear of abandonment
    Fear of failure
    Fear of feeling guilt
    Fear of feeling shame
    Fear of criticism
    Fear of failure
    Loss of respect—from others or self

Loss of youth and vitality
Loss of good physical health
Loss of good emotional health
Divorce
Unhappiness
Loss of control
Other (specify): _____

Once again, for each rating equal to or higher than 3, write a short paragraph or two elaborating on the nature and characteristics of your worry or fear.

Protecting Your Vulnerabilities

Now you have a greater awareness and understanding of your own deepest needs and strongest fears and worries. In this way, you have a good idea of how a manipulator might get control over you. The key issue, of course, is for you to sort out the "good guys"—the nonmanipulative people who truly have your best interests at heart—from the manipulators. Here's the basic rule: Love, friendship, and goodwill generally *feel* safe and uncomplicated; whereas manipulation *feels* coercive, confining, and entangling.

If a skilled manipulator holds out the promise of something that you deeply desire or something that you deeply desire to avoid, he or she is very likely attempting to throw a hook into your need system. Eventually it can become a deep hook if you take the bait.

If the manipulator then shows you how your behavior or actions can either help to make this gain occur or can help to prevent a feared loss (this is the bait), the seed of manipulation is planted, and unless you act to resist his or her control, your personal freedom may well be at risk. Your most desired gains and your most feared losses are precisely where the manipulator will attach the hooks that will increasingly pull your strings.

Remember, at first the manipulation may be camouflaged as "benign influence," but once the manipulation shifts to coercion and the pressure starts to build, the manipulator can hold powerful sway over you. This is why it is important to be honest with yourself when reviewing the lists earlier in the chapter. By knowing what you really desire and/or what you most fear losing, you are gaining an edge over a would-be manipulator who tries to exploit those deeply felt desires of yours. Knowing what they are allows you to keep your antennae raised so that you are in a better position to spot manipulation when it is on you.

9

The Mechanics of Manipulation

A S ANYONE who has been victimized by a manipulative relationship knows, manipulation is a *process* that takes place over a prolonged period of time. If it came about swiftly in a new relationship, the mark would immediately catch wise and likely end the relationship before it began. "Slow and steady" could be the mantra of many manipulators.

As was pointed out in previous chapters, the manipulator uses levers of control over the mark—either the promise of something to *gain* that the victim needs or strongly desires or the promise of *avoiding loss*—activating the victim's worries and fears that something he or she strongly wishes or needs to avoid will occur unless there is compliance with the manipulator.

The rules of manipulation are relatively simple at their core. When gain is promised, the basic formula is "If you do what I want, I will reward you with [whatever the promised gain is]," or "If you don't do as I ask, you won't get what you want and need." In both these scenarios, the mark does not currently have the desired object. This is the proverbial carrot.

However, when *threat of loss* is the control lever, the formula shifts to coercive control: "If you *don't* do what I want, you will *lose* what you value or desire or already have, or another negative consequence will take place." And this is the stick.

The manipulator does not necessarily verbalize the formula explicitly; it is often in the form of a veiled threat. However, whether it is verbalized or not, the carrot (the gain) or the stick (the loss or the punishment or consequence) lies at the core of *every* manipulative relationship. If you think that you might be in a manipulative relationship now, ask yourself, "What is the rule that governs this relationship? How does [the manipulator] control my behavior?" In other words, ask yourself, "Am I here in the relationship, or am I doing this thing [some act or behavior] out of my own free will and accord, or is it because I fear losing what I have?"

The Manipulative Shift

Very often the manipulator will use *both* levers of control either simultaneously or sequentially. For example, early in the manipulative process, the manipulator may hold out the promise of a major gain to the mark. As the process progresses, the lever of control may subtly or insidiously shift to the prospect of losing the promised gain or losing even the opportunity for gain. Once the manipulative control shifts to a threat of loss, the manipulation feels coercive and increasingly stressful.

Generally, the promise of a major gain and/or the threat of a major loss represents a kind of end point or goal in the relationship. On the way to that goal—be it a gain or avoidance of a major loss—the manipulator controls his mark tightly with smaller, more frequent, and more routine manipulations along the way. It is in the exercise of these frequent manipulations that the mark increasingly loses a sense of control, feels manipulated, *is* manipulated, and eventually becomes coerced and highly stressed. And if the promised gain never materializes, the mark also will correctly feel deceived, especially when she has been compliant with all the demands put on her.

For example, if the promised gain is a job promotion, a manipulative supervisor might exercise control over his subordinate that might be expressed in requests that she work overtime and on weekends, that she do special favors or projects for the supervisor, or that the subordinate break or bend certain corporate rules or spy on her coworkers for the supervisor's benefit. Each of these individual manipulations is controlled by the immediate reward or punishment that follows compliance or noncompliance. However, the overall major lever of control by the manipulator over the victim remains constant: "If you do what I want, you will get promoted and get ahead in the company. If you don't and you displease me, you won't be promoted [or other bad things may happen]." Implicit in the latter rule are such threats as demotion, job loss, negative performance reviews, criticism, or humiliation in front of other employees.

In Chapter 2 we saw Francine initially controlled by her desire to be successful and earn a lot of money. As the manipulation progressed, the control lever shifted to her fear of losing the promise of the profitable partnership that Arnie threatened.

The Manipulative Process

The fact that manipulation occurs as a process over time means that there is actually a string or series of promised gains or threatened losses used to control the mark's behavior. The manipulation is rarely one isolated event; it is an evolving process over time.

Manipulators control their marks through the use of systematic patterns of positive and negative reinforcement or reward, as well as actual or threatened punishment or negative consequences. The insidious process of manipulation generally begins with the manipulator baiting the trap through subtle, indirect, or even deceptive means. Or the process may begin with the manipulator's use of pleasant, appropriate, or benign signals of reward.

Having first aroused the mark's interest, the manipulator will seek to elicit compliance and cooperation with what may appear to be harmless or unimportant requests. Often, in the beginning phases of a manipulative relationship, the requests or desires of the potential manipulator may seem fully in line with the mark's own self-interest. In fact, when the mark—who does not yet realize that she is about to become a victim of manipulation—perceives this link between the manipulator's interests and her own, the critical step of establishing trust between the manipulator and the mark is begun.

Of course, this trust will erode over time as the true nature of the manipulation is increasingly revealed.

Having aroused the mark's interest, the manipulator will seek to elicit compliance and cooperation with his requests, needs, or desires. The mark—who is not yet a full-blown victim—may feel flattered and even seduced by the manipulator's attention and interest.

However, the initial "buy in" by the mark to what appears on the thin surface to be a positive relationship in which both parties' needs will be met steadily progresses to full ensnarement in the manipulation trap. For example, a new and potentially manipulative boyfriend initially may reward desired behavior from his girlfriend with signs of affection, verbal praise, or other indications of approval. Over time, the rewards may shift to promises of long-term commitment or references to the possibility of marriage and family, much like the story of Valerie and Jay in Chapter 2.

When the boyfriend begins to use the threat of breaking up or expresses his sudden "need for space" or talks about his struggle with ambivalence and uncertainty about the relationship, the shift from relatively benign or seemingly harmless influence to coercive control and manipulation occurs. Now, instead of the promised gain (e.g., matrimony), the girlfriend is manipulated by the fear of loss— loss of the relationship, of his love, of the possibility of marriage, and of family. Just the *threat of loss* is sufficient to leverage his control over the girlfriend's actions as well as her thinking, perception, and diminishing self-esteem. If in her mind she had done something to bring about the negative change in the manipulator's mood, she will hasten to comply with his next request for fear of replicating that same response in her boyfriend that almost had him walking out the door.

This is *classic* manipulation.

Now let's explore the five major methods manipulators use to achieve power and control over their marks.

Methods of Manipulative Control

Manipulative relationships characteristically appear complex and complicated, especially to the marks. However, the methods that manipulators use to leverage and control the behavior of their victims actually can be understood in fairly simple terms.

Once you understand the basic methods of control, you will be able to penetrate the complicating verbal snares and emotional webs that manipulators spin and to see in clear and simple terms just how the manipulator is exercising his or her control. This is vital to being able to break the hold a manipulator may have on you—even if the manipulation has been ongoing for some time.

There are five basic ways that manipulators control their victims. They are

1. Positive reinforcement
2. Negative reinforcement
3. Intermittent or partial reinforcement
4. Punishment
5. Traumatic one-trial learning

In psychological terms, these are basic modes of learning. As such, they are not limited to manipulative relationships. In fact, these basic modes of learning are used to influence, teach, coach, motivate, discipline, encourage, and manipulate behavior across all kinds of relationships and situations.

Whether you are aware of these methods or not, you have no doubt used them to modify, influence, shape, or control the behavior of other people, and they have no doubt been used to influence, shape, and control your own behavior. We teach children, train employees, change our spouses, and encourage or discourage our friends and families using these basic methods.

So what is different about manipulation? Before I answer this question, let's look at each of the basic methods of control first.

Positive Reinforcement

This is the basic principle of reward. If you like what someone is doing and you want to increase the frequency and consistency of the desired behavior, you provide a reward, or positive reinforcement, for it. This reinforcement may come in the form of praise, money, approval, affection, gifts, attention, facial expressions that connote approval or pleasure (e.g., a smile or laugh), public recognition, and a myriad of other material and nonmaterial rewards and their symbols that people use to reward or reinforce one another, such as money, title, and promotions.

Positive reinforcement is the fastest way, for example, to train a dog to sit or stay. Positive reinforcement means that when the dog does what she is supposed to do during training, she gets a reward, such as a pat or a dog biscuit.

Human beings, from infancy on throughout our lives, are highly influenced by the rewards or reinforcements given to us by those on whom we depend, whom we love, whom we respect, and who are in a position to provide the gains we seek and to prevent the losses we dread. In hundreds of interactions each day, all of us reinforce others and receive reinforcement from others for the things we do. Positive reinforcement increases the likelihood that the desired behavior will occur again.

It is important to note that positive reinforcement generally feels good—it is a pleasant experience for the target. This is why it works. We like to earn our boss' approval or praise, to receive affection or just to see happiness on the faces of those we love, and to be told that we are appreciated and valued or that the effort we have made matters. A skilled manipulator knows this and will tend to use positive reinforcement to make the target feel good (and, by association, well disposed toward the manipulator who is delivering the reward) and to strengthen desirable behaviors and habits.

Do manipulators use positive reinforcement? Absolutely—especially in early phases of the relationship. And if they stopped with only the use of positive reinforcement, especially if the rewards given are gains you desire, the relationship would not be manipulative. In fact, relationships that are based on positive reinforcement are generally pleasant and enjoyable.

The feedback, subjectively, is that the target perceives that her behavior is pleasing to the manipulator. For people-pleasers in particular, this can be enormously rewarding—and the "pleasing" behavior is frequently and often compulsively repeated.

However, after the manipulator lures the target into a relationship using frequent or continuous positive reinforcement, the "game" often shifts in an important direction. Instead of frequent, relatively small rewards, a substantial and much-desired gain is now proposed—either directly or indirectly. But the gain appears *just beyond the reach of the target*. Initially, the target is highly motivated to attain the gain. Being able to delay gratification, the target is willing to do what is necessary to earn the desired reward and will wait patiently until the time comes for the "big gain" to be achieved.

Here's the rub, though: In manipulative relationships, the gain remains elusive and seemingly unattainable. Nevertheless, the manipulator *continues* to hold out the promise of the gain as a motivator for the target. Eventually, as the dynamics of the manipulation become clearer, the target begins to suspect that the promised gain likely will never materialize no matter how hard or ardently he or she tries.

Thus, while the target frustratingly struggles to understand what is happening, another subtle shift moves the reinforcement mechanism—or lever of control—from positive to negative. Under the manipulator's control, the target feels more compelled by the *fear* that the gain may never be reached than by a straightforward drive toward the goal. Now the *need* to avoid the loss (of a gain that has not yet been earned) is the driving motivation.

Negative Reinforcement

Many people confuse this form of reinforcement with punishment but it is very different. The best way to grasp how negative reinforcement works is to use a laboratory example. Picture a cage set up for a laboratory rat. (Learning psychologists do a lot of their research with these creatures.) The cage is divided into two compartments: One part is painted all black—walls, floor, ceiling—with the exception of a white door that connects the black compartment with the other half of the cage, which is painted entirely white—floor, ceiling, walls. To demonstrate both positive and negative reinforcement, let's say that the purpose of our study is to teach (influence, coach, manipulate?) our rat to move from the black part of the cage to the white compartment as quickly as possible.

Rat 1 is placed in the black compartment. In the white compartment, at the farthest end from the black section, we place a hunk of cheese. The rat will investigate the black section for a little while until it finds the white door, which it will push open out of curiosity and, very likely, because of the scent of the cheese coming from the other side. It will then enter the white compartment and promptly eat the cheese, thereby receiving positive reinforcement. The rat is happy.

The same rat is then placed in the black section a second time. This time, in far less time than the first trial, the rat will push open the white door and, once again, be rewarded (positively reinforced) with the delicious hunk of cheese. The rat is now happy and smart.

We do this exercise a few more times. Each time the rat will go through the white door into the white compartment in less time than the previous trial. Even if we omit the cheese altogether, the rat will continue to move promptly from the black to the white compartment because the white section has taken on some positive quality to the rat just through the association of the cheese with the white section.

So far we have demonstrated how to teach a rat to move from the black to the white compartment entirely through positive reinforcement—the presentation of a reward immediately after the rat has done the desired behavior (gone from the black to the white cage).

Now let's put rat 2 into the black part of the cage. Our purpose is the same—to see how quickly the rat will learn to move from the black to the white section. However, this time there is no cheese in the white compartment. Instead, the floor of the black compartment is electrically wired and is set to deliver moderately painful electric shocks in response to the slightest pressure. Thus rat 2 is placed in the black compartment and is instantly experiencing a highly unpleasant electric shock. Within seconds, the rat will begin quite literally bouncing off the walls, shaking, urinating, and doing a lot of other behaviors that highly stressed, anxious rats display routinely. However, in its bouncing, the rat sooner or later will bounce into the white door, which will lead it into the white compartment where *there is no shock*. There is no cheese; but the painful, unpleasant experience stops as soon as the rat goes through the white door.

Rat 2 has experienced negative reinforcement—the presentation of a painful, unpleasant, or otherwise negative stimulus or experience that is stopped, turned off, or discontinued after the desired behavior is performed.

By the way, it may not surprise you to learn that rat 2 learns to move from the black to the white part of the cage even faster than rat 1. And once the behavior is learned or acquired, the rat will continue to throw itself through the white door into the white compartment even when the shocks are turned off in the black compartment. Now the black section has acquired secondary negative qualities through association with the shock.

Negative reinforcement is sometimes known as *aversive conditioning*—the "reward" is the avoidance or stopping of an aversive experience when the subject (in our case, the rat) complies with the nasty experimenter's desires.

Now let's consider the human analogues to positive and negative reinforcement. As we draw these parallels, the profile of the manipulator may begin to take form.

As explained earlier, there are innumerable examples of positive reinforcement in our daily experiences. We commend our children for doing a good job or for getting a good grade or trying their hardest in an athletic game. We thank our employees or offer praise when they do the job we desire. We compliment or show appreciation to our friends for favors rendered or other desirable behaviors. We are especially affectionate toward and appreciative of family members when they do something that is generous, kind, thoughtful, or otherwise desirable.

The examples of positive reinforcement are endless. And for the most part, people who are positively reinforced or rewarded are inclined to repeat the same or similar behaviors in the future and tend to be relatively happy or content in their roles—as long as they feel that the reinforcement is adequate or appropriate to their efforts.

What are the human analogues of rat 2? Consider the mother of a typical 12-year-old with a messy room. She tells him repeatedly to clean his room; when he does not comply, she ratchets up the level and starts yelling, then threatening to impose harsher punishments if he does not move his you-know-what and clean his room. Finally, when the boy complies, the nagging, yelling, and threatening stop. She does not tell him what a fine, good boy he is or reward him. She merely stops yelling. Voilà! Negative reinforcement.

Nagging is the human equivalent of shock grids to the rat. Withholding communication (the silent treatment) is a form of negative reinforcement. Breaking the silent treatment depends on the other person complying with the desired behavior (e.g., an apology or doing what was asked). Anytime that one person subjects another to a painful, unpleasant, or otherwise negative experience *until* the other complies with a request, demand, or need, negative reinforcement is at work.

Other human analogues to the shock grids include the manipulator's use of such negative reinforcers as sulking, nagging, whining, playing victim or the injured or hurt party, or crying or blaming others. These tactics, when effective, arouse feelings of guilt, shame, unmet obligation, or shirked responsibility.

Alternately, the manipulator may use intimidation tactics such as yelling, swearing, threatening, or displays of temper or anger to control the target by arousing the target's fear of disapproval, fear of anger and confrontation, or fear of rejection or abandonment. Or the manipulator may make unfavorable, invidious comparisons between the target and another person (e.g., a sibling or a coworker) to stimulate unpleasant feelings of low self-esteem, low self-reliance, and feelings of inadequacy.

Finally, the manipulator may stir up the target's ambivalence or fear of change or of making a bad decision or making a mistake merely by questioning ("Are you really sure of what you want?") or expressing generalized uncertainty ("You just never can know things for sure.").

These negative feelings—guilt, fear, and inadequacy—activated by the manipulator's tactics are intensely uncomfortable, just as the shock is to the rat. By acquiescing, complying, or capitulating to the manipulator's demands or requests, the target can bring immediate (but only short-acting) relief from the painful or unpleasant feelings and fears. By doing what the manipulator wants, the target's actions are *negatively* reinforced by the stopping, albeit temporarily, of the uncomfortable, unpleasant, or painful sensations.

Now you can begin to see a clearer outline of the manipulator. Fear or worry of a potential loss or other negative consequence (e.g., "If I don't do this work, I'll lose my job," "If I don't give this kid my homework to copy, I won't be popular," "If I don't let him or her control the relationship, he or she will leave me") clearly fits the description of an aversive stimulus that can be stopped—at least temporarily—when the desired behavior is done.

Manipulators often use negative reinforcement. Remember that rat 2 was compliant but not at all happy. People who are manipulated or controlled through aversive conditioning and negative reinforcement typically become resentful, angry, and frustrated, and they begin to experience a downward spiral of depression, low self-esteem, anxiety, and other negative symptoms that perpetuate the aversive experience.

Turn back and take a look at the case studies in Chapter 2. See if you can label positive and, more important, negative reinforcement in the stories.

Intermittent or Partial Reinforcement

Both positive and negative reinforcement can be given on either a continuous and consistent basis or on an intermittent, partial, randomized, and unpredictable basis. These two schedules of reinforcement—the pattern of frequency and predictability of the reinforcement—have a great deal to do with how the mark feels about the person who is delivering the reinforcement and about the behavior that is generating it.

When positive reinforcement is delivered on a partial or intermittent schedule, the stage is set for the development of addictive behavior. The very uncertainty built into a randomized schedule can create frustration and compulsive behavior where the target is always looking for that anticipated reward. In manipulative relationships involving intermittent or partial reinforcement, the target has great difficulty differentiating between circumstances where behavior is being partially and intermittently reinforced and those where the reinforcement (gain) has ceased altogether.

Invariably when I work with patients who are in manipulative relationships, I find myself telling them what I refer to as "The Pigeon Stories." Actually, this is really another laboratory demonstration of the effects of continuous versus partial reinforcement.

This time the subject is a pigeon instead of a rat. The cage (sometimes called a *Skinner box* after the behaviorist B. F. Skinner) has nothing in it other than a lever that the pigeon can poke with its beak and a food trough for delivering pellets of pigeon food. Let's look at continuous positive reinforcement first.

Pigeon 1 enters the cage. We have kept the pigeon off food for a little while so that it is good and motivated by hunger. The pigeon will just poke around the cage for several seconds until it pokes the lever just out of curiosity or accident. As soon as the bird pokes the lever, a pellet of pigeon food is delivered to the trough, which the pigeon immediately eats.

Pigeon 1 has been positively reinforced for pressing the lever. Our goal is to teach the pigeon to press the lever, so we continue to reward the lever pressing on what psychologists call a 100 percent continuous reinforcement schedule. This simply means that each and every time the pigeon presses the lever, it gets a pellet of food. One press, one pellet. Within no time, pigeon 1 will develop a strong lever-pressing habit.

Okay. Now we leave pigeon 1 and move onto pigeon 2. Its experience in the cage begins just the same as that of pigeon 1. Once the lever-pressing habit is established—after 10 or so presses and pellets—we suddenly and without warning change the game. Instead of rewarding or reinforcing the bird 100 percent of the time on a continuous basis, we begin to randomize delivery of the pellets, only rewarding the pigeon for lever pressing part of the time and then on a wholly random, unpredictable basis. This is sometimes referred to as a *gambling schedule,* otherwise known as intermittent or partial reinforcement.

Thus pigeon 2 might press the lever six times in succession with no pellet of reward, and then, on the seventh press, it gets a pellet; then 19 times without reward, followed by pellets every other press for 6 lever presses; then 15 times with no reward, followed by a pellet; and so on. The point is that the reinforcement comes on an unpredictable basis, only *part* of the time. No rhyme, no reason.

To demonstrate the effects of these two reinforcement schedules, we stop rewarding both pigeons altogether. No more pigeon food pellets for either. And we use a stopwatch to see how long each bird will continue to press the lever without any positive reinforcement. Psychologists consider this an analogue to compulsive, self-defeating behavior because there is no payoff or reward.

Pigeon 1 continues for a relatively short while. Because it got food previously for each and every press, it is apparently relatively easy for the pigeon to tell that the good stuff—the reward—for pressing the lever is now over. And it simply slows down and soon stops lever pressing altogether. After all, what is the point?

However, in the next cage, pigeon 2 continues to press that lever—without any reward—until the bird eventually collapses with fatigue. Why? Because the reward came now and then, unpredictably, the bird apparently cannot tell that the game has changed from intermittent reward to no reward at all. In effect, pigeon 2 has become *addicted* to pressing the lever. In human terms, hope springs eternal in the heart of someone conditioned with intermittent reinforcement.

Psychologists have demonstrated that birds, rats, and people who are rewarded with a partial, random, or intermittent schedule of reinforcement develop addictive or compulsive behavioral habits. Just picture a person standing in front of a slot machine for hours and hours, if not days. The gambler keeps pulling that lever, losing money most of the time, until every now and then the gambler hits a jackpot. The jackpot is the "fix"—the reward that sustains the compulsive desire to keep gambling for the next win.

Again, what is the human analogue to partial reinforcement, especially in the context of manipulation? Consider a woman who becomes romantically "addicted" to a destructive love relationship with a manipulative partner. In the beginning of the relationship, the man showered her with attention, affection, generous gifts, and the like each and every time she showed him the desired behavior (sexual attention or doing favors for him). Over time, however, he becomes less and less forthcoming with the rewards. In fact, he becomes downright unpredictable. She can knock herself out doing nice things for him, and he will act bored or otherwise entitled to the favorable treatment. Once in a while, though, with no predictable pattern, he will reward her with telling her he loves her or by being affectionate or kind. He keeps her hooked by rewarding her only intermittently. She is pigeon 2.

Alternately, consider the executive assistant (let's say a young man) who works for a woman chief executive officer (CEO). The CEO is a brilliant dynamo but is known to have a nasty and unpredictable temperament. Eager to get ahead, the assistant puts out a major effort to please his demanding boss. At first, she is pleased and praises him quite frequently. Then she simply ignores his efforts. Periodically, however, and unpredictably, she comes into the office in a fiercely ugly mood. She snaps, yells, and berates him all day until he does whatever it is that pleases her, and then she merely stops. He becomes conditioned (manipulated) by partial or intermittent *negative* reinforcement.

Thus, with both positive and negative reinforcement, the schedule or pattern of reinforcement is a key factor in establishing control of another's behavior. The consistency of continual reinforcement—even if it is negative—produces far less anxiety and stress in the recipient than unpredictable, random, or intermittent reinforcement.

In fact, if you want to *create* anxiety and stress in a subject, the most effective approach is to deliver a painful or otherwise highly unpleasant stimulus or experience on a random, unpredictable basis. This is exactly what terrorists do. Think of the nation's anxiety following the September 11 terrorist attacks. We are always waiting for the "other shoe" to drop.

Some manipulators are outright psychological terrorists in that they keep their victims on a constant razor's edge, never knowing if or when the next aversive experience will happen. It is the *uncertainty*—rather that the bad event per se—that breeds anxiety and stress.

Punishment

The only difference between negative reinforcement and punishment has to do with the timing of the negative experience. With negative reinforcement, the unpleasant stimulus occurs *before* the target produces the desired behavior, and discontinuation of the unpleasant, aversive stimulus (the reinforcement) depends on the compliance of the subject. While manipulators and others who use negative reinforcement rarely verbalize the formula behind their method, it is clear: "I will do this unpleasant thing to you until and unless you do what I want. If you comply, I'll stop the aversive experience. If you don't, the bad thing or thing that you don't like will continue and maybe even get worse."

With punishment, the negative experience is a *direct consequence* of undesired behavior on the part of the subject. This time the rule is, "If you do something that I do not like or want, I will hurt you."

Punishment is used widely as a disciplinary or control mechanism. However, what most people do not realize is that punishment is actually far less effective in controlling behavior than either positive or negative reinforcement. In fact, instead of eradicating the undesirable behavior, punishment generally produces erratic behavior—sometimes the undesirable behavior persists, and sometimes it stops temporarily, only to reappear later in the same or a different form.

Interestingly, when punishment *is* effective, it is usually because the subject has learned the connection between the negative behavior and the negative consequence. As a result, the subject learns to *fear* the punishment—and the fear itself becomes a kind of negative reinforcer. The fear exists, and the subject tries to *avoid* the punishment or negative consequence not only by stopping the undesirable behavior but also by replacing it with a desired behavior that, in turn, lowers the subject's fear of an actual negative punishment. Thus the lowering of the fear that follows the desired behavior becomes a negative reinforcement.

Manipulators establish coercive control of their victims often by using punishment in combination with other methods of reinforcement.

Traumatic One-Trial Learning

The fifth way that manipulators control their targets is through traumatic one-trial learning. This method of controlling behavior is the proverbial "hand on a hot burner" event. In other words, you do not need a second experience to learn to keep your hands away from a hot burner if you have experienced a painful burn once.

A terrifying or traumatic experience can produce long-term and generalized effects. For example, a child who is attacked and bitten by a pit bull is very likely to develop a morbid fear of dogs that may last a lifetime. The generalization effect means that the child's fear attaches not only to pit bulls but to dogs that resemble pit bulls in any way or maybe even to all dogs in general.

The clinical syndrome of posttraumatic stress disorder (PTSD) can develop after an individual is exposed to a single but highly traumatic event in which he or she may have witnessed or experienced serious injury or death of others and/or experienced a strong fear of his or her own death. Often a PTSD victim will experience feelings of helplessness, shock, and horror in response to the event. A defining feature of the syndrome is the reactivation of the fear response to future occurrences that resemble the traumatic event directly or even symbolically.

The terrorist attacks of September 11 gave nearly everyone in the country a sense of traumatic exposure. Even people who were not near ground zero or anywhere else in New York City experienced trauma by virtue of watching the horrific images live—and then in endless repetition—on television. That experience allowed people thousands of miles away to experience the event almost as if they had been there in person.

But how do manipulators use traumatic one-trial learning? A physically or emotionally abusive husband, for example, generally can establish fear and trepidation in his victim after the first traumatic episode. Thereafter, the victim is fearful and adopts a response style designed to try to avoid another occurrence of abuse. Unfortunately, almost every abuser continues to reexpose his victim to repeat attacks that serve to deepen the impact of the initial traumatic experience.

One of my patients was a young woman in a training program with a new company. She was ambitious, smart, and highly motivated, and at the time she took the new position, she was already establishing a name for herself as someone likely to succeed in a competitive sales environment.

Toward the end of her initial training, after having received rave reviews from nearly all her mentors, she was assigned to a new trainer. After just a week or so on the new assignment, her new supervisor called her into his office, closed the door, and proceeded to attack her verbally in personal and vitriolic ways. His tirade lasted a full 10 minutes, during which he pounded on the table for emphasis, repeatedly raised his voice to a loud yell, and turned red in the face, all the while demeaning, criticizing, and berating her.

Immediately after this experience, the young woman began sobbing and shaking and had to leave for the day. She stayed home for the rest of the week. When she returned to complete her 3-month assignment, she remained terrified of engaging the anger of her explosive mentor. Despite her efforts to try to make sense out of his criticism, she could find no direction or logic in his remarks. And after he exploded, her anxiety and shock interfered with her ability to really listen or "hear" his words anytime in the future.

Instead of the aggressive, motivated trainee she had been previously, the woman adopted a "low profile" just to avoid even being noticed by her abusive trainer. This "under the radar" mode caused her sales figures to drop radically. Moreover, her anxiety and stress compromised her performance and diminished her confidence. In just one traumatic tirade, the trainer had accomplished his mission: manipulative control over the emotions and behavior of the young female trainee.

While verbal and even physical aggression is a common method of manipulators, extreme emotionality and/or loss of emotional control can have a very strong impact.

A male patient of mine had been happily dating a woman for a few months until, quite unpredictably from his vantage point, she totally "lost it" and erupted in an "emotional hurricane." He reported that she ranted incoherently and that she cried, screamed, sobbed, and escalated into a full-blown panic attack. And to top it off, she somehow blamed it all on him.

After that episode, he continued to date the woman for a few more months. But, he explained, "It was never the same.

I walked on eggshells around her, fearful that I was going to trigger another one of those meltdowns. I never want to be around that kind of craziness again."

The psychological term is *one-trial learning* because the impact on the victim is so strong as to effect behavior control, often through the instigation of fear and intimidation, almost immediately. However, people who erupt emotionally or physically generally do not stop with one episode—their own self-control is not that good. In other words, if the meltdown happened once, it is a safe bet that it is only a matter of time before the other shoe drops with a blood-curdling thud.

Multi-Method Manipulation

Most manipulators use most or all of the methods just described to establish and maintain control over their victims' behavior. Methods are not mutually exclusive—the manipulator may change tactics and methods just to remain unpredictable and confusing to his or her mark.

The Big Lie

A final method of manipulation is the "Big Lie." As we have discussed, the manipulator's control is often based on the promise of a big gain or the avoidance of a big loss, fear, or another negative, dreaded event. Once the victim has bought into the promise or expectation of gain or avoidance of loss, the manipulation game is afoot. And the manipulator may use all the methods of reinforcement and control described earlier to keep the victim complying with what the manipulator wants all along the way to the supposed big gain or avoidance of the big loss.

All too often, what victims discover is that the promise or expectation was never going to materialize even if the compliance was near perfect. As one victim of a manipulative boss explained, "I was never going to get that promotion. It did not matter what I did for him. He was lying to me the whole time in order to keep me under his control. At the end of the two worst and hardest-working years of my life, I got laid off. That was my big reward! I only wish I had realized early on that the whole thing was a big con game."

Victims of romantic manipulation are convinced that if they do what the manipulator wants, they will earn and maintain his or her love and commitment and, conversely, that if they fail to please the manipulator, they will lose the love and eventually be abandoned. Again, sadly, the victim discovers that the person who is exploiting and manipulating her does not really love her in the first place, so the threatened loss of love was a Big Lie all along.

The good news about discovering that you have been conned by the Big Lie is that this awareness can be quite liberating—and can form the first step toward freedom from manipulation.

The Victim's Countercontrol

Finally, I cannot conclude a chapter on manipulative methods without explaining that the target of manipulation can have reciprocal control over the manipulator. Here's how:

Once a coercive manipulative pattern is established, the target of a manipulative relationship experiences a great deal of stress, anxiety, internal conflict, and distress over the loss of control he experiences. As a result, the victim rarely recognizes his own role as a collaborator in the manipulative process. Moreover, because he *feels* controlled and relatively powerless, the target often cannot see or feel where his own countercontrol lever lies.

Remember, it takes two (at least) to have a manipulative relationship. We have seen in this chapter how a manipulator can engage his mark or target in a relationship through relatively benign or even pleasant positive reinforcement and the promise of a desired big gain down the line.

And we have seen that, over time, the method of control often changes from positive to negative reinforcement and aversive conditioning. Both continual and intermittent reinforcement schedules are used, as are punishment and even traumatic one-trial learning.

However, it is critical to recognize and appreciate that the victim is also controlling the manipulator, albeit in a far less conscious or intentional way. Each and every time the victim complies and produces the desired behavior (or ceases an undesired behavior), the manipulator is, in turn, reinforced for using manipulative methods. Remember the discussion earlier in this chapter about rewards in the section on positive reinforcement? Well, every time the victim complies with the manipulator's "request," the manipulator is receiving *his* reward, or positive reinforcement.

Over time, the victim comes to think of herself as "under the thumb" of a manipulator. The stress of the experience has predicable and distorting effects on the mark's perception, judgment, and self-esteem. Most important, the stress limits the mark's ability to perceive alternatives or to adequately identify the true range of her personal autonomy and freedom. The net effect is a deepening of the malicious process of manipulation and a downward spiral of depression, anxiety, and lowered self-esteem.

As the victim weakens and succumbs to the manipulator's control, the latter becomes stronger and more assured of the effectiveness of his methods. Manipulation is a form of emotional blackmail. Once you give into blackmail, you reinforce the blackmailer's methods.

The first step in freeing yourself from manipulation is recognizing that you are not as powerless as you feel. By enabling the manipulator to control you, you are exercising a kind of power and control of your own. *If you stop complying with the coercion, you will cripple the effectiveness of the manipulator's methods.* Your compliance only serves to reinforce the manipulation. However, as you will soon learn, your resistance eventually will weaken the manipulator's hand and loosen the emotional ties or bonds that have controlled you.

Does resistance mean that you will suffer the negative consequences that you fear? Will a coercive manipulator merely raise the ante of unpleasantness in order to pressure you into compliance in a negative reinforcement strategy? Yes, initially, the manipulator is likely to balk at your newfound resistance and to even escalate his or her coercive tactics. However, with continued resistance, the manipulator will be forced to change either his or her tactics or choice of victim. Manipulation only continues when it is effective.

In the next few chapters we will see how emotionally unhealthy it can become for a victim to submit to the coercive control of a manipulator. Fully understanding the impact of manipulation will help you to answer these critical questions:

1. Is the price you are paying emotionally by allowing a manipulator to control you really worth it?
2. Are you truly avoiding a *worse* consequence—the big loss or the loss of the big gain—by colluding in the manipulation?
3. Is the anxiety, depression, stress, and damage to your self-esteem and self-respect even worse than the consequence you have been trying so desperately to avoid?

10

Are You in a Manipulative Relationship?

B Y THIS POINT you may strongly suspect that there is a manipulator in your life, maybe even more than one. You may have recognized telltale personality traits or tuned into some of the methods and tactics a manipulator is using. And you have taken a close look at aspects of your own personality—your buttons and hooks—that may make you vulnerable to a manipulator's exploitation.

Ideally, these insights and information have already helped you to steer clear of certain people before they ensnare you in a manipulative trap. Realistically, however, you may already be ensnared and even deeply involved with a person who has gained control over you in a way that is causing you to feel concerned, if not downright unhappy.

Victims of manipulation develop a characteristic set of feelings about themselves as a result of colluding in the toxic dynamic. The good news about this is that the clues and indicators of whether you are likely involved in a manipulative relationship are inside of you. The best place to look is at your own feelings and reactions to the relationship.

Here's a quiz that will help reveal whether you are participating in a manipulative relationship. First, identify the name of the person with whom you are currently having issues, problems, or difficulties that may well signal manipulation. Remember, the people in your life who have the most direct impact on the things you most want—the big gains— or the things you most want to avoid—the big losses or fears—are the ones most likely to manipulate you effectively. They are often

- Family members
- Spouses or romantic partners
- Coworkers, subordinates, and especially superiors at work
- Friends/social relationships
- Academic relationships
- Members of social groups or organizations that are important to you
- Professional relationships

Are You in a Manipulative Relationship?

(Repeat this exercise for each person.)

Think about your relationship with _____.

Read each statement, and rate how strongly you agree or disagree with it. Mark your answers at the end of each statement or on a separate piece of paper.

5 = strongly agree
4 = agree somewhat
3 = agree slightly
2 = disagree somewhat
1 = strongly disagree

1. I often feel that I just do not know how to make _____ happy.
2. I sometimes feel confused and unclear about what _____ really wants.
3. It mostly feels to me that _____'s needs dominate our relationship.
4. I often wind up feeling more to blame for problems in my relationship with _____ than he or she does.
5. I feel that _____ does not understand my needs in this relationship.
6. I sometimes feel resentful and angry toward _____.
7. I rarely express my negative feelings to _____.
8. I sometimes feel that _____ has more control over my feelings and behavior than I do.
9. I sometimes feel that _____ is using or exploiting my giving nature.
10. More and more, I feel dissatisfied and frustrated with the way _____ treats me.
11. I believe that I am much better at meeting _____'s needs than the other way around.
12. I often feel that I have to choose my words very carefully around _____.

13. I say and do things to try to avoid angering or upsetting _____.
14. I sometimes feel that _____ takes me for granted.
15. Instead of expressing my anger directly toward _____, I often direct my anger inward and wind up feeling bad about myself, sometimes even depressed.
16. When I think about my relationship with _____, I realize that I do not feel as good about myself as I once did.
17. I'm not sure that _____ really has my best interests at heart.
18. I often feel that I need _____ far more than he or she needs me.
19. I sometimes feel that I am trapped in my relationship with _____ with no clear way out.
20. I am better off checking first with _____ about a decision or action than relying on my own judgment and risk making a big mistake.
21. I often feel that _____ has more control over my feelings and behavior than I have over his or her feelings and behavior.
22. I worry frequently about upsetting, disappointing, or letting _____ down.
23. I often feel that something bad will happen if I do not do what _____ wants.
24. No matter how much I do for _____, he or she has a way of making me feel that I have not done enough.
25. I have sometimes thought that _____ intimidates me with his or her anger, moods, or emotionality.

26. I often feel in my relationship with _____ that I do not have much freedom to really be myself or to do what I really want.
27. _____ has a very strong influence over how I feel, think, and/or act.
28. I do not feel that I can do much to change _____.
29. Even when I do something that really pleases _____ or makes him or her happy, the good feelings never seem to last very long.
30. I work much harder at this relationship than _____ seems to.

How to Score Your Answers

First, add the numerical value of your answers. Your total will range from 30 to 150.

How to Interpret Your Answers

If your score is between 120 and 150, you are quite likely to be involved in a manipulative relationship. The closer your score is to 150, the greater is the negative emotional toll that that relationship is taking on you. The pattern of behavior you have developed is actually rewarding the manipulator and enabling his or her control over you to continue and very likely increase.

If your score is between 100 and 119, you are developing signs of being manipulated. Remember, manipulative relationships rarely change unless the victim stops enabling the process to continue.

If your score is lower than 99, you are not likely to be the victim of manipulation in this relationship. The difficulties in your relationship are likely to have other explanations.

If your score is in a danger zone, focus on this: Manipulators are rarely motivated to be the first to change in the relationship. The paradox of manipulation is that the person who feels least powerful—the victim—is really the one who can become most empowered to make changes.

Remember, manipulation is used because it *works*. Your score reflects just how well the manipulative methods are working to control you in the relationship. As I have discussed previously and will again soon, the most effective way to thwart and/or change a manipulator is by changing your own responses so that the manipulation *no longer is effective.*

You will learn to use effective resistance tactics that will disrupt, derail, and ultimately destroy the manipulator's ability to coercively control you. And you will learn to "harden the target" by making yourself less vulnerable to manipulation now and in the future.

Before we turn to the strategies to counter manipulation, you need to understand in more depth why and how a manipulative relationship affects the victim. Only when you realize how unhealthy your participation is will you be fully motivated to change.

11

The Impact of
Manipulation

I N THE 25-PLUS YEARS that I have been
practicing clinical psychology, I cannot recall a single instance where a patient sought
my help because he or she wanted to stop manipulating
other people. On the other hand, not surprisingly, victims
of manipulation frequently seek psychological help to
cope with a relationship that is a source of great frustration and stress to them.

Generally, by the time the victim is sufficiently distressed
to seek help, he or she bears clear signs of the manipulator's
control. The "honeymoon" or initial period of relatively
benign influence typically has long passed, and the manipulator has tightened the strings of coercive control. Sometimes
the victim knows full well that manipulation is at play and
that he or she is caught in a web partly of his or her own making. Other times, however, the victim lacks clarity on the true
nature of the manipulative dynamic in which he or she is
enmeshed.

Footprints in the Snow

Either way, the victim characteristically complains of feelings of confusion about what the manipulator's desires and motivations really are. In the context of the relationship, the victim often reports feeling unhappy, highly stressed, and full of anxiety and worry. Subjectively, victims often feel quite "out of control" in terms of their own behavior and emotions, only sometimes recognizing that the manipulator is really pulling their strings.

In effect, while the mark or victim may not yet have clarity as to the manipulative dynamic or to the role he or she plays in the collusion, an experienced clinician certainly can read the "footprints" left by the manipulator all over the victim's emotional state. In this sense, while the manipulator may not be present for the therapy (although somewhat later he actually may join in the therapy process, albeit usually reluctantly), his or her identity is recognizable from the proverbial "footprint left in the snow" or, more accurately, on the victim's psyche.

The Silent Contract

There is often an implicit or silent agreement between the manipulator and the victim not to speak directly about the "rules" of their relationship. Part of what the manipulator controls is what will and will not be permissible communication in the relationship. This is often accomplished simply by being unwilling or unavailable to participate in a given conversation (e.g., "I'm not in the mood to talk about this" or "I don't have time now to discuss this").

Nonverbally, the manipulator simply may convey his or her displeasure by ignoring a comment or question, walking out, ending a phone call, or otherwise indicating that he or she is not receptive to discussion.

It does not take long for the silent contract to be set. Communication, especially as it pertains to the power and control dynamics of the relationship, is limited or forbidden. The threat of conflict and confrontation looms large to the victim for even suggesting that manipulation is taking place. Thus the silent pact continues.

I hear many similar stories from frustrated patients who ultimately report being stymied by this type of manipulative wall. However, it usually takes a while for the victim to realize what has been going on in the relationship.

When threats are implicit, no direct responses are tolerated. In fact, the potency of the implied threat, coercion, or intimidation lies in the victim's inability—or *perceived* inability—to talk about the fact that he or she feels *manipulated.*

As long as the real agenda of the manipulator is kept hidden or obscured, the pattern will persist. By controlling and limiting communication, the manipulator creates mounting frustration and eventual hostility in the victim. However, without a vehicle for expressing the negative feelings, these feelings often become internalized, thereby contributing to the process of emotional harm to the victim.

The Emotional Toll of Manipulation

In Chapter 10 you had a chance to evaluate the likelihood that you are participating as a victim in a manipulative relationship. If your score is in the danger zone, you are very likely experiencing the negative emotional impact of manipulation.

Being manipulated means that you are ceding control over your own feelings, actions, and even thoughts to someone else. Although a manipulative relationship may begin with and even explicitly recognize a big gain as its goal or purpose, the positive character of the control almost invariably shifts to a coercive or negative basis over time. Once manipulation takes hold, the lever of control is more closely related to the fear or threat of losing the promised gain or to the threat or fear of another dreaded or undesirable loss or other negative consequence.

Recall from Chapter 9 on the mechanics of manipulation that negative reinforcement—also known as *aversive conditioning*—while very effective in controlling behavior, does not produce a happy or well-adjusted subject. Negative reinforcement, punishment, and traumatic one-trial learning are, for the most part, fundamentally coercive in nature. And few people enjoy being coerced into much of anything.

If the manipulation includes unpredictable or randomized partial reinforcement—you are never quite sure when a reward or a cessation of a negative experience (negative reinforcement) is going to happen—the very strong and unpleasant component of anxiety is added to the victim's experience. The lack of predictability creates high uncertainty that, in turn, produces anxiety.

Thus manipulation is both coercive and anxiety-producing. And it is highly frustrating, which, in turn, creates hostility and anger. These are toxic feelings that begin to take a substantial emotional toll on the victim.

However, there are other signs and symptoms that victims of manipulative relationships develop. Characteristically, victims frequently feel responsible for causing these negative feelings and reactions in themselves. The self-blame becomes a major feature of victim status.

A closer look at the way manipulation operates, though, will help you to understand that the negative feelings are understandable and largely even inevitable reactions to the stress and frustration caused by the manipulation.

Let's take a look at some other common emotional reactions to being victimized by manipulation.

Confusion About the Manipulator's True Motives

The confusion that develops in the victim about the manipulator's motives is often an integral part of the manipulative control. Recall that the endgame for the manipulator is to advance her own self-interests and goals with little or no regard for those of other people. However, a skilled and clever manipulator will disguise her actual motives, often with disarming and effective reassurances, such as "You know I only want you to be happy" or "I have only your best interests at heart" or "I am on *your* side—I'm trying to help you out."

The victim's confusion is magnified many times over when the manipulation occurs in the context of a family/marital/romantic relationship. In such relationships, there is a general expectation that love and altruism will prevail over the self-centered goals of manipulation. You may not *expect* those who say they love you to manipulate and exploit you, so you are likely to use the defense mechanism of *denial* to protect yourself from painful—although ultimately necessary—realizations. But some of the most painful experiences of manipulative relationships that I have seen have, in fact, occurred in families.

Sometimes the victim's confusion lies with the manipulator's carefully disguised motives. Other times the victim's own denial and fear keep him from recognizing the manipulative methods being used to control him. In such cases, the victim is often deeply entrenched and enmeshed in a sustained manipulative pattern before he becomes fully aware of the negative toll the manipulation is taking on his emotional and often even physical health.

For example, in family or marital relationships, the expectation or assumption of love can fog an accurate perception of the manipulation that really exists. "I know that my husband really loves me," a depressed wife who had been victimized by emotional abuse and manipulation for years once told me in a therapy session. "But I am just a constant disappointment to him."

Such a victim also illustrates the erosive effects of manipulation on self-esteem. Frequently, as in this case, these erosive effects can cause the victim to internalize the blame and to see herself as the main reason that the relationship is problematic. When working with patients in this category, helping to rebuild their shattered self-esteem is usually a top treatment priority—even before helping them deal with the manipulators in their lives.

Confusion about what the manipulator "really means" or "truly wants" is the inevitable result of maintaining the silent contract to keep the manipulative agenda hidden or obscured. When direct communication—especially about the power and control dynamics of the relationship—is avoided, the most effective tactic for clarification and for ending or reducing confusion is crippled.

Confusion is also prevalent in relationships where the formal power structure is reversed by the manipulation. For example, parents often do not recognize that their child is manipulating them; or a supervisor or boss may be slow to realize that a subordinate actually has taken over the reins of control.

To the extent that the manipulator uses randomized or partial reinforcement as a means of control, confusion, stress, and anxiety are increased by the uncertainty and unpredictability inherent in the reinforcement schedule.

Finally, it is imperative to remember that manipulators are generally quite capable of lying. If it serves his or her purposes, a manipulator may well seek to disguise his or her motives simply by lying about them.

Frustration and Dissatisfaction with the Relationship

As the vice of manipulation tightens, the victim typically feels increasingly frustrated and dissatisfied with the way the relationship makes her feel. Victims often report feeling unable to make a manipulator happy no matter how hard they try.

Of course, since the manipulative relationship, by definition, serves the needs of the manipulator, the victim will become increasingly frustrated and dissatisfied over time as the volume of her unmet needs grows. When needs are not met, they become *more* exaggerated and pressing—not less.

Victims who try to change the relationship but remain unsuccessful in doing so are understandably frustrated. If the victim connects her self-worth to the manipulator's willingness or unwillingness to change, erosion of self-esteem is the outcome. "If he really loves and values me, he'll change" and "If I show her how good I am at this job, she will treat me differently" are examples of familiar refrains that many of my patients have played for me over the years.

Psychologically, frustration leads to hostility and aggression just as surely as night follows day. Even though the victim may suppress the mounting anger, fearing negative consequences if she were to risk direct expression to the manipulator, the toxic emotional and physical consequences of heightened hostility levels still take their toll. Research has long shown that sustained and/or frequent hostility has damaging effects on cardiovascular health, raising the triple threat of stroke, heart attack, and arteriosclerosis (i.e., blockage and hardening of arteries).

Sense of Imbalanced Power and Control

While victims often express confusion about the motives or methods of manipulators, they tend to be well aware that there is a significant discrepancy, asymmetry, or imbalance in the power and control dynamics of the relationship. They generally can acknowledge that the other person—the manipulator—holds the reins of control in the relationship. Even my patients who have trouble at first acknowledging this know intuitively that something in the relationship is out of whack—or, more accurately, out of balance.

Victims also perceive that the manipulator's needs dominate the relationship while their own remain largely unexpressed, unacknowledged, and consequently, unmet.

The victim's sense of the imbalance of power and control in the relationship reflects the reality of manipulation. It is important to note that many of the buttons that make victims vulnerable to manipulation in the first place also help to establish and reinforce both the perception and the reality of the manipulator's dominant control.

For example, people-pleasers and those with a near addiction to approval from others are predisposed to put the needs of others first. Victims with an external locus of control and those who are reluctant to rely on their own independent judgment are psychologically predisposed to perceive and even to create relationships in which others exercise far more power over them than the other way around. In effect, they become willing accomplices in their own manipulation.

Whether the victim knowingly or, more likely, inadvertently colludes with his own domination by the manipulator, the negative emotional impact is essentially the same. In addition to the confusion, frustration, hostility, and dissatisfaction just described, victims also report feeling exploited, misunderstood, demeaned, or taken for granted. They also express feeling controlled and/or out or control. Eventually, victims feel depressed, demoralized, stressed, worried, and anxious.

Diminished Self-Reliance and Lowered Self-Esteem

Manipulative relationships serve the ego demands of the manipulator and chip away at the self-esteem of the victim. As the manipulation continues, the insidious unraveling of the victim's healthy self-reliance picks up speed.

The more the victim succumbs to the control of the manipulator, the less he will be able to perceive himself as an autonomous, independent, and self-reliant adult. Consequently, both the victim's self-respect and confidence diminish as manipulation persists.

Despite the fact that the victim's needs remain in the deep back seat of the relationship, he will at the same time become increasingly dependent on the manipulator or on the relationship and what it represents (e.g., his job or career, the family, the commitment to the relationship itself).

The victim's diminished self-respect, enhanced dependency, and growing sense of helplessness and loss of control combine to form a dangerous formula for the development of clinical depression.

Resentment and Anger Toward the Manipulator

As political history has amply demonstrated, people who are manipulated, controlled, and exploited—especially by coercive dictators unwilling to spread or share power—eventually rise up in anger and rebellion. However, long before that anger is expressed openly in battle or protest, it goes underground, where it feeds the passion and plans of resistance and revolutionary fighters.

The analogy to interpersonal manipulation, exploitation, control, and curtailment of freedom and independence is apt. When your personal freedom and autonomy are abridged by a manipulator's tight control, frustration ensues, and the twin fuses of anger and aggression are ignited.

However, just as resistance fighters initially operate as an organized underground, the victim's anger may well be contained in the emotional underground as well. Said another way, the victim may be suppressing the anger that the manipulation is creating rather than violating the silent contract and/or risking a confrontation or negative reaction from the manipulator.

There are serious risks to allowing another person to create high levels of stress for you. Dr. Hans Selye, the father of modern stress theory in medicine, advised that the greatest danger from stress was from that caused by another person. In fact, Selye strongly cautioned that you should cut such stress-producing individuals out of your life.

At the core of the harmful stress reaction that manipulators cause is the fomenting anger that often has no direct outlet of expression, at least not toward the person who seems to be the cause of the frustration and hostility. Lacking such an outlet for direct expression, the victim is likely to redirect the stress in ways that may have further harmful consequences.

For example, one of my patients redirected her anger back onto herself, which produced feelings of self-blame, guilt, and depression. Another patient channeled his anger into a dangerous level of physiologic arousal, thereby putting himself at greater risk for a host of physical illnesses and problems. In your case, you may be exacting a toll on your other relationships—outside your relationship with the manipulator—by transporting and displacing the suppressed anger into irritability, impatience, excessive criticism, or other signs of ill temper.

Entrapment and Victimization

As we have seen, manipulative relationships create stress for their victims for many reasons. Whatever the cause, the net effect of living with high, damaging levels of stress is that it feeds a vicious, self-perpetuating cycle.

Because it is coercive, often unpredictable, and inevitably frustrating, manipulation creates stress that is underscored by anxiety and/or depression. The stress has predictable distorting effects on the victim's perception, thought, and judgment. Specifically, stress closes off the victim's ability to see alternatives, to perceive avenues of exit, or even to try effective challenges to the status quo. The victim may see only two courses of action: Either I do what he wants, or I face intolerable, devastating consequences.

The victim feels trapped—ensnared in a pattern of manipulation—and cannot envision a viable way out. In fact, the victim only *perceives* that she is trapped in the manipulative relationship because her own negative thinking traps her. Negative thinking distorts and magnifies the downside of projected outcomes or consequences, often into full-blown catastrophes.

Further, the victim gets trapped in a self-image of *victimization*. This means something more than that a victim feels like a victim. Victimization is a harmful pattern of thinking and behaving characteristic of people whose victim status has been fully incorporated into their self-concepts. And it represents the damaging effects on your emotional functioning of seeing yourself as a victim.

The psychological profile of victimization includes a pervasive sense of helplessness, passivity, and loss of control; pessimism and negative thinking; and strong feelings of guilt, shame, self-blame, and depression. This way of thinking can lead to hopelessness, despair, and even giving up on the possibility of making things better or different in the future.

In short, manipulation is harmful to your emotional health because it creates and perpetuates your feelings and self-perception as a victim. The more victimized you feel, the less capable you will feel to free yourself from the toxic pattern. And the longer you collude with manipulation by complying with the manipulator's requests or demands, the deeper your sense of entrapment in the manipulator's web of control.

There is still another way in which manipulation insidiously operates to perpetuate itself. Remember the seven emotional buttons that make you vulnerable to manipulation that you learned about in Chapters 2 and 3? Briefly, they include:

1. People-pleasing habits and mind-sets
2. Approval addiction

3. Fear and avoidance of anger, conflict, and confrontation
4. Lack of assertiveness and an inability to say no
5. The vanishing self: blurry identity and unclear personal boundaries
6. Low self-reliance
7. External locus of control—a person's belief that the main cause of things that happen to him or her is more in the control of other people or of other outside factors (e.g., luck) than under his or her own control

These particular needs and personality styles set you up as a mark or natural target for manipulators. And, as you have probably realized, these buttons can develop as the *consequence* of participating as a victim in a manipulative relationship.

What this means is clear: When you persist as the victim of a manipulative relationship, you become diminished emotionally in ways that *make you even more vulnerable to this and to other manipulative relationships* now and in the future.

Breaking Free from Manipulation: Trust Yourself

As a victim, you probably already have the painful knowledge that manipulation has weakened your autonomy, sensitized your fears, and skewed your thinking negatively. To begin the process of reclaiming control over your own life and breaking out of manipulative patterns, you will need to rely on the one person that the manipulator has trained you not to trust—*yourself.*

This takes commitment and determination. As long as you struggle to please the manipulator, gain his approval, and avoid anger and confrontation at almost any cost, your self-reliance will remain impaired. This is exactly what the manipulator wants. If you distrust yourself, you are far more likely to remain under the manipulator's thumb while he pulls all your strings. The manipulator wants you to be weak and dependent. More than anything, the manipulator intends for you to continue doing what he wants.

However, by reading this book, you are connecting with a very different self—the self that wants to reverse or change the harmful collusion of manipulation and regain your self-respect, healthy autonomy, and self-esteem. And you want to get rid of the negative emotions—stress, anxiety, and depression—that your victimization has induced and perpetuated.

How do you begin to trust yourself after feeling so unempowered for so long? Trust is very often a leap of faith. You need to make that leap and decide to trust yourself because you are the main change agent in your life.

As long as the manipulation is effective—and *you* control whether or not to reinforce the manipulator's strategy by either complying or resisting—the manipulator has no motive, need, or desire to rock the boat and change the way your relationship works. *But you do.*

You now know that by *not* changing yourself, you will only tighten the vice of the manipulator's control. You also will open the door wide and invite even more manipulators into your life. And you realize the negative impact on your emotional and physical health as well as the collateral damage to other relationships from the stress you are enduring now.

What you do not yet know is *how* to change yourself. Rest assured that you will learn what you need to do to break free of manipulation in the remainder of this book. From this point forward, think of yourself as a *former* victim—as a person *who used to get manipulated.*

Starting now, you are in training to become an effective resistance fighter against the manipulators in your life. You are fighting for nothing less than your personal freedom, your emotional and physical health, and your self-respect and integrity.

Take the leap. Then turn the page.

12

Resistance Tactics

ANIPULATORS can invade your personal territory in virtually any interpersonal realm. If you are (or ever have been) the target of a manipulator, you know from painful personal experience that capitulation and compliance with the manipulator's control will only strengthen the emotional stranglehold in which you are caught.

Once the dynamic of manipulation is in motion, it will gain force every time you give in or yield to the manipulator's will. Left unchallenged, the manipulator will overcome and subjugate your freedom, your autonomy, your integrity, and even your self-esteem.

The insidious nature of manipulation creates feelings of helplessness, loss of control, and dependency in the target. You must isolate and label these self-defeating emotions as precisely that—feelings, *not* facts.

The *fact* is that you are not without power in this relationship, even if you are the marked target. The resistance tactics you are about to learn will disrupt, derail, and ultimately even destroy the manipulator's ability to control you. These proven tactics will afford you the means and methods of your *countercontrol* over the manipulator.

Do not worry about how to directly change the manipulator; this is *not* within your realm of control. It is also a common mistake made by people who are tired of the manipulation trap. Save your strength; it will not work. Just focus on *changing yourself*. This is something that is well within your powers. Always keep in mind that manipulation is used because it *works*. It follows, then, that the most potent way to thwart a manipulator is to *change your responses* so that the manipulator's tactics are no longer effective.

Your power lies in your ability to *resist* the pressure and to *foil* the finesse of the manipulator's aims and purposes. It is time to end your collusion with manipulation.

To Resist or Leave, That Is the Question

If you are caught in a web of interpersonal manipulation, your immediate goal is to stop participating as a compliant victim who yields to pressure and capitulates to insidious, coercive, or unfair tactics of control. There are two approaches to this goal: (1) resistance and/or (2) extraction (leaving the relationship altogether). In a turn of the tables, both approaches comprise the *countercontrol* that you will now exercise over the manipulator.

Resistance

Resistance tactics work much like metaphorical molasses—when poured on, will slow down, gum up, and otherwise cause the mechanism of manipulation to malfunction and, ultimately, to stop altogether. In the immediate face of effective resistance, manipulators may first attempt to raise the ante by tightening the strings of manipulation. However, when you do not succumb to the increased pressure—which you *will* learn to resist—the manipulator is left with only two workable alternatives: He or she can adapt to the changes *you* have made by developing healthier, more respectful, and more balanced forms of interaction and influence at least with you, and/or he or she simply may tire of the resistance and choose instead to manipulate another vulnerable target whose capitulation and control are far less difficult to achieve.

When you resist manipulative pressure successfully, you recalibrate the power balance in the relationship. You must realize that this shift in the power equation inevitably will alter the relationship and the behavior of both parties involved. Do not be afraid of this change.

Since you will initiate the changes and *will* hold your ground, the manipulator can choose either to adapt to your lead or else remain stuck in a strategy that no longer works, at least as far as the relationship with you is concerned. You must keep your eye on the prize: By remaining clearly "on message"—that the old manipulative methods will *no longer* effectively work to control you—you can reclaim your freedom, autonomy, self-respect, integrity, and self-esteem. This is absolutely a battle worth fighting *and* winning.

Realize, however, that this may be a scary and emotional time for both of you. Even if your resistance tactics succeed in producing a new repertoire of healthier, nonmanipulative responses from the other person, there likely will be a rocky adjustment period. When the fundamental dynamic of any relationship undergoes change—even if the change is very much for the better, as in this case—the adjustment period can be somewhat difficult. Take comfort in the fact that the difficulty eventually will yield to a far healthier and balanced interdependence.

Realistically, there are limitations to the use of resistance. What if the resistance tactics do not produce adaptive changes in the manipulator's behavior toward you? Some manipulative relationships are too ingrained, too unhealthy, and even too abusive to correct. And many manipulative personalities—particularly those that comprise full-blown personality disorders, as discussed previously—simply do not and will not change.

For such individuals, manipulation of others is their modus operandi—their immutable way of functioning. When you proclaim your independence from manipulation by effectively resisting coercion and pressure, the manipulator's response simply may be to change partners and continue dancing. If you will not play the game, the manipulator will find a more vulnerable target who will.

Remember, manipulators use manipulation because it works. Stop helping them.

Extraction

After some deliberation, you may be the one to decide that the best and healthiest thing for you to do is to disconnect from the relationship altogether. The emotional damage done by the manipulation may be well beyond the point of repair. Recalibrated or not, the relationship may not be sufficiently valuable or beneficial to warrant the effort of a resistance struggle.

In such cases, extraction, or removing yourself from the relationship altogether, is the ultimate resistance. Severing a relationship—even one that is unhealthy—may involve sadness and other painful emotions. However, when the terms of a relationship demand that you maintain your status as a compliant victim of manipulation, the pain of ending it is significantly reduced. Clearly, a relationship that requires you to compromise your self-esteem, freedom, and integrity is not in line with your self-interests. Whatever the ostensible bond—family, friend, boss, lover—your continued participation in a relationship that mandates manipulation and compliance is simply not good for you.

There are *worse* consequences than leaving or losing a relationship altogether. Certainly losing yourself in the fog of manipulation—losing sight of who you are and what you value, need, and believe—would be a truly dire outcome. Remaining a victim of manipulation, diminishing your self-respect or integrity, and losing your self-esteem are far too high a price to pay for holding onto the elusive or illusory security that such a relationship may represent.

Finally—and this is important—if your unwillingness to be manipulated costs you a relationship, what did you really have in the first place?

Small-Scale Efforts

If the manipulative relationship—or the manipulator—will not adapt to the healthy changes in your behavior, or if it simply is not worth preserving, extraction may well be the best method for ending your role in the manipulation.

There are some manipulative relationships, though, where the limitations of your countercontrol are imposed by circumstances. In certain instances, for example, such as those involving close relatives, where blood ties are strong and complicated, or work relationships, where your livelihood and long-term career options are at stake, extraction simply may not be feasible, at least not in the near term.

When leaving is not an option and dramatic personality change on the part of the manipulator just is not in the cards, you may need to focus your resistance on *small-scale efforts*. In such circumstances, your autonomy and self-esteem will be regained incrementally, measured in small steps, quiet or even silent protests, and minor victories. Since extraction from these particular relationships may not be possible or ultimately desirable, your full freedom from the manipulative relationship may have to be postponed, deferred, or even redefined. But do it on *your* terms.

One of my patients was in a vicious manipulative relationship with her mother. All attempts by my patient to talk to and reason with her mother had failed. My patient was a grown woman with three children, yet her mother never stopped treating—and manipulating—her like the child she had not been for more than 30 years. In this case, complete extraction was not an option. However, by learning and implementing key resistance tactics, my patient was able to redefine the relationship so that the manipulation—while still attempted—fell flat most of the time. Using the resistance techniques that I am about to teach you, my patient was able to deflect many of the attempts at manipulation in a way that rendered it essentially impotent. The mother still tried to manipulate her daughter—and sometimes her daughter chose to comply—but each attempt became a bit harder for the mother than the time before. Soon the frequency of the manipulative attempts eased up, although they never stopped completely. But my patient had redefined the relationship— and the manipulation—in a way that she could live with.

Seven Key Steps to Resist Manipulation

Now it is time to learn the *tactics of resistance* so that your countercontrol can begin. You will be altering *your behavior* first, even before you work on changing your thinking and ultimately changing the negative feelings that propel you toward capitulation, thereby fueling and refueling the manipulation cycle.

As you will see, the steps are cumulative in the sense that they build on one another. The more steps you use to countercontrol the manipulator, the more potent your resistance will be. But each step has a kind of potency of its own, and putting even one resistance action into motion will increase your sense of control and reduce your feelings of victimization and helplessness. Remember, when you take steps to make the manipulation less effective or ineffective altogether, you will exert your own pressure back on the manipulator to change his or her tactics and/or to find another target to manipulate instead of you. Either way, you wind up healthier and happier.

Some of the steps may not be appropriate to your specific relationship or circumstances. This is for you to determine. The important point is that you now have viable options—things that you can do instead of meekly giving in and reinforcing the toxic pattern of manipulation.

Step 1: Playing for Time

Manipulators exert pressure through various means to force you into compliance with what they want you to do. They may use active means to apply compliance pressure such as becoming angry, yelling, name-calling, door slamming, and other bullying tactics; or they may choose passive means such as sulking, pouting, crying, the silent treatment, ignoring, or other quieter ways to exert pressure.

Until now, you may have learned to comply with a request quickly—even immediately—thereby short-circuiting the manipulator's pressure tactics altogether. Or if the manipulator uses pressure tactics, you probably have capitulated because such tactics create pain and/or discomfort for you, and you have learned through negative reinforcement that the immediate pain will cease (the yelling will stop; the silent treatment will yield) when you give in and do the manipulator's bidding.

The problem is that when you do so, not only is your compliance behavior reinforced, but the manipulator's pressure tactics are also reinforced because you give in to what he wants you to do. This situation creates a substantial power imbalance tilted in the favor of the manipulator.

The first step of resistance is to break that pattern and, in so doing, to recalibrate the power balance of the relationship. You will do this by inserting a period of time between the manipulator's request or demand and your response. Once you learn to build in *time to think* about your options, your sense of control will increase immediately. When you can make the manipulator live by your timetable instead of his, you take back power.

Since you may be in the bad habit of automatically complying or agreeing to your manipulator's requests or demands—agreeing or saying a fast knee-jerk yes before you have given yourself any time to think about them—you will need to break this habit. The best way is to take an immediate breather after the manipulator expresses her request.

Telephones lend themselves easily to the insertion of a breather. If you are speaking on the telephone and a manipulator (or a potential manipulator) asks you to do something or go someplace, your *immediate* response should be something such as:

- "I need to put you on hold for a minute or so. Excuse me/thank you."
- "I have to ask you to hold the line for a minute. Thanks."
- "I need to put the phone down for a minute. Excuse me."
- "I'm going to have to call you back in a few minutes. Thank you."

Notice that you are *not asking permission*. Instead, you are informing the manipulator that you *will* be taking a minute away from the telephone. This breather allows you to prepare your next statement, which is a play for time (see below).

Face-to-face situations require a bit more finesse, but they will still permit you to take a breather in order to break the automatic compliance habit. Excusing yourself from the scene of the interaction for a few minutes is all you will need to interrupt the tendency to immediately say yes or agree to something you would rather avoid. Leaving the scene, if only for a few minutes, is the live equivalent of putting a telephone caller on hold.

After the request has been made but *before* you reply, excuse yourself for a few minutes to use the bathroom, make an urgent phone call, get something from your car or office, get some coffee or water, or any other reason you can think of to leave the manipulator alone with her request or demand for a few minutes.

Whether you put the caller on hold or leave the scene of a face-to-face request or demand, your purpose is to take the breathing time to do just that. Breathe deeply through your nose, and exhale through your mouth for a count of 20. Do not breathe quickly, or you may start to hyperventilate. Your goal is to calm yourself down and to focus on your next move, which is to play for time.

Here are some sample phrases that will stall the manipulator's request or demand:

- "I need some time to think about what you are saying. I'll get back to you just as soon as I can."
- "This issue deserves some real consideration, so I'll need a bit of time to think it over, and I'll let you know as soon as I can."
- "I can't give you an answer right now. I will certainly think it over, and I'll get back to you as soon as possible."
- "I'm not in a position right now to answer that, but I will get back to you when I am."
- "This is an important issue, and I will need some time to give it the thought it deserves. Then, of course, I'll get back to you."

You should write down each of these phrases and make at least two copies—one to keep by your telephone and one to keep in your wallet. In this way, the phrases will be available for your review during the short breather period.

You may use one or more of the phrases listed, or you may add more of your own design to the list. The key component is that you are *telling* the manipulator that you are not complying on his timetable. Also, you are not asking permission. While it may be more polite to ask, doing so will cede power and control back to the manipulator. Your purpose is to reset the power balance so that it is more equalized.

It is important that you become comfortable and facile at delivering these phrases. You should practice the phrases out loud in front of a mirror. Before you begin practicing, focus for several seconds on this thought: *"I have every right to think before I commit myself to doing anything for anybody."*

Smile pleasantly as you say each phrase; this will help you to keep your tone pleasant but still assertive. Say each phrase at least five times; repeat the exercise three times a day until you are sure that you sound firm, direct, and sure of yourself as you play for time. Remember that you are not *asking* for time; you are informing the other person that you *will* be taking some time to reflect before you respond. Take care not to raise your vocal inflection at the end of the declarative sentence as though you were asking a question.

After you have practiced all the phrases, select at least two that you feel are most appropriate. Commit them to memory. Continue to rehearse them out loud in front of a mirror or, if possible, with a supportive friend or a therapist. The more you rehearse, the less difficult the phrases will be to actually say to the manipulator.

Do not expect to be perfectly calm and self-assured when you first play for time with the real manipulator. Realistically, you will very likely feel anxious, maybe even fearful. Just let the feelings be there and say the phrases anyway. Focus on *doing the resistance behavior* by saying your selected phrase.

At this point, do not worry about how you feel inside. It is normal for you to feel uncomfortable because you are altering ingrained patterns with someone who is a big source of difficulty and stress in your life. Most important, do not let your feelings drive your actions. This is what you have been doing all along—complying with the manipulator's demands because the intimidation, fear, pressure, and other manipulative tactics have been unpleasant.

You now know that whatever respite the manipulator gives you when you comply is short-lived at best. Soon, he or she will be creating the familiar discomfort in order to manipulate you into compliance with yet another request or demand.

Only you can break the vicious cycle. You must determine to sever the negative reinforcement link by changing your behavior from compliance to resistance. As you will soon learn, there are other more effective and long-lasting ways to change your negative feelings without succumbing to the manipulative pressure.

Take comfort in the fact that your feelings *will* change as your behavior changes. But you must *do the behavior first, and your mind will follow.* As you continue to resist the manipulation, your negative feelings eventually will transform into pleasant, even exhilarating feelings of relief, empowerment, and most of all, freedom.

Step 2: The Broken Record

Naturally, you can expect the manipulator to object to your play for time. After all, you are dealing with a master of pressure and coercion. However, since you control the objection or challenge, you will be prepared to deal with it *without explaining yourself and without giving in.*

It is critical that you do not become engaged in a conversation with the manipulator about *why* you need time, *what* you are going to think over, or *when* exactly you will be ready to respond and do what the manipulator wants. If you get pulled into this morass, you will lose control.

The manipulator will raise objections precisely because she expects to talk you out of your position and push you into your characteristic compliance, but, you are now too smart to fall for this ploy. However, you *will* need some kind of a response because the manipulator is likely to turn up the heat and start using pressure tactics to gain your compliance.

The response technique you will use is called "the broken record." This is a simple but powerful method for standing your ground. There are two components to the broken record:

1. Acknowledge that you hear and understand the manipulator by accurately labeling the *emotion* or *feeling* that is being expressed.
2. Repeat your play-for-time phrase just like a broken record.

This is it. You will not—and should not!—enter into an explanation, question-and-answer session, or discussion of any *content* of what the manipulator is saying. Remember, if you start talking too much, you will lose control. Resistance is the name of the game—not debating or arguing your position, however in the right you feel.

But you should keep foremost in your mind that you *are* absolutely in the right to state that you want to think before you act. The manipulator may have been pulling your strings for a long time, but you are *not* a puppet. You are a self-determining human being, and you have now decided to cut the strings.

Here is how the broken record sounds. The following script is actually from one of my patients who used it successfully with a close friend who was constantly manipulating her into running charity events at her daughter's school. It shows you how to put the two components together to fend off success-fully the pressure to comply.

> **Manipulator:** "You're so good at organization that I've decided to let you plan the entire party."
>
> **Target (my patient):** "I need to put you on hold for a moment. Excuse me." [Takes a breather and quickly rehearses the play for time.]
>
> **Target:** [Returning to the call.] "Thanks for holding. You know I need some time to think about this. I'll get back to you as soon as I can."
>
> **Manipulator:** [Sounding incredulous.] "Think about what? Are you telling me that you might not do the party?"
>
> **Target:** "I understand that you feel surprised [acknowl-edges the manipulator's expressed emotion], but I need to think about this, and I'll get back to you."
>
> **Manipulator:** "Well, I can't wait very long. In fact, there isn't much time as it is, which is why I need you to do the planning. I really need an answer now" [sounding exasperated].
>
> **Target:** "I understand that you are anxious, but I need time to think about it. I'll get back to you just as soon as I can."
>
> **Manipulator:** [Angry now; raises voice.] "You're being completely unreasonable as usual. I really need your help, and you are leaving me out here in the cold. What's your problem? What do you need to think about? I want to know!"
>
> **Target:** [Takes a deep breath to calm down.] "I under-stand that you're frustrated, but I'll have to get back to you about this later."

Manipulator: [Yelling now.] "Are you just going to keep saying the same stupid thing?"

Target: "I understand that you're angry, but I do need time to think about this."

Manipulator: [Tight-lipped.] "Fine. Why don't you do just that. Think about it and get back to me with your answer that you are going to do this party. There's no point in talking anymore. Good-bye."

Target: "Good-bye."

The broken record will work with even a determined manipulator, as it did in this case. At the end of the preceding conversation, observe that the target—my patient—does not give in to her impulse to apologize for making the manipulator angry. Nor does she rise to the bait of any of the manipulator's questions. She merely follows the formula of first identifying, as accurately as possible, the emotion or feeling the manipulator is expressing ("I understand you feel [emotion]"); then she repeats the play-for-time phrase just like a broken record.

The best way to prepare for using the broken record is to run through some practice scripts that you write. You will find that writing scripts that are true to form for the manipulator in your life will greatly aid your preparation and increase your sense of control. By predicting what the manipulator is likely to say—which you *can* because you have dealt many times with his or her tactics—you will be armed and ready with your broken-record responses.

Try to enlist the help of a supportive friend, family member, or therapist who will role-play with you. You can use the scripts you have written, and you can improvise with your role-playing partner. Ask the person who plays the part of the manipulator to really push you to capitulate. The more practice you have using the broken record to resist manipulative pressure, the better prepared you will be for the real thing.

As you practice, ask for feedback from your role-playing partner on your posture, eye contact, voice stability, volume and tone, and overall appearance. Work on developing a delivery style that conveys an impression of contained strength and confidence. Again, do not worry about how you feel inside; your goal now is to refine your behavioral presentation so that you can *act as if* you are self-assured and focused on achieving your resistance goals.

Practicing, rehearsing, and role-playing the resistance tactics have yet another benefit. By exposing yourself to practice situations, you *inoculate* yourself to the stress that the real interaction with the manipulator likely will produce. And the more realistic the practice scenario is, the greater is the inoculation and stress-reducing effect.

However, you should not expect to eliminate the stress entirely. To do so not only would be unrealistic but also actually would be counterproductive. Your practice conversations will help you to cope far better with the stress that does occur when you are talking to the manipulator directly. In fact, psychological research shows that performance actually is enhanced when stress levels are contained at moderate levels— as opposed to too high or too low.

Ideally, then, the practice experience should help to keep you "pumped up" sufficiently to be energized and motivated. At the same time, the inoculation effect should help to prevent your stress levels from skyrocketing and disrupting your ability to think or speak effectively. With practice, you will become better able to gauge where the boundaries of the optimal moderate range are for you.

Step 3: Desensitizing Anxiety, Fear, and Guilt

To resist manipulation effectively, you must learn to tolerate some pretty uncomfortable feelings. Until now, the fuse on your negative emotions has been far too short. As a consequence, when the manipulator lights your fuse by making you feel anxious, fearful, or guilty, it burns down very quickly—sometimes nearly immediately—and triggers the capitulation and compliance that fuels the manipulation cycle.

The desensitization technique you are about to learn will help you to withstand the negative feelings without resorting to your old habits of giving in to the manipulator's demands.

First, let's define our terms. *Anxiety* is the experience of fear without an object. What this means is that anxiety is a rather abstract and generalized variant of fear. Unlike fear, anxiety is not directed at or connected to a specific outcome or consequence. When you feel anxious, you may worry about many different things. Often one worry trips off another and then another, building to a cascade of anxious thoughts. Anxiety makes you feel subjectively nervous, pressured, and unfocused.

A manipulator may trigger your anxiety by pushing your insecurity button or triggering your self-doubts. Anxiety levels are raised by uncertainty. Manipulators do this by making vague and ambiguous references to something negative that may (or may not) happen in the future. And anxiety can be ramped up by negative feedback or criticism that injures your self-esteem or by subtle yet invidious comparisons between you and someone else that the manipulator seems to prefer.

Fear, though, is connected to a specific outcome or consequence. Manipulators intimidate their targets into submission by arousing fear. Some of the typical fears that a manipulator's tactics arouse include:

- Fear of disapproval
- Fear of abandonment
- Fear of anger
- Fear of conflict and confrontation
- Fear of change or making a mistake
- Fear of rejection
- Fear of isolation

Both fear and anxiety are easily conditioned. This means that after you have been exposed to these negative feelings as a result of the manipulator's effective tactics, you may develop fear and/or anxiety reactions just to being in the presence of the manipulator even when he is not explicitly activating these feelings.

Guilt is a uniquely human emotion. It is the result of feeling *excessively* responsible for the emotions and/or experiences of others. If you are vulnerable or have a well-pulled guilt string, a skilled manipulator can send you on a rocket-propelled guilt trip headed for a destination of capitulation and compliance.

A manipulator may display emotionality to show you how unhappy she is and to make you feel responsible for creating the distress. The manipulator may cry, sulk, pout, or play the victim or martyr. She may complain of stress-related physical pains and problems for which you are somehow responsible because you have done something—or failed to do something—that has caused the manipulator to become emotionally upset. Guilt can even be induced with a certain facial expression (e.g., looking hurt or wounded) or with a vocal tone or inflection.

If you are a people-pleaser, you may well feel guilty when you even *think* about saying no to a request from another person. Once a manipulator hones in on your emotional hot button, he needs to do very little to control you with guilt. The manipulator does not have to do the work; you do it all for him.

The manipulator(s) in your life may use one, two, or all three negative emotions to intimidate, coerce, and control you. Regardless of whether anxiety, fear, or guilt is used, your reaction to your own discomfort is flawed. Simply put, when you detect the negative feelings, you label the experience as intolerable, as something that you cannot stand or bear, and therefore as something that must be eliminated or at least curtailed as soon as possible.

When you feel anxiety, fear, or guilt, your response mechanism is propelled into an emergency mode as though a three-alarm fire were raging uncontrolled. The manipulator merely hands you the fire hose and points you in the direction of capitulation and compliance with her desires. The urgency you feel, however, results from the manipulator's pressure *and* from your overreaction to the discomfort that you *feel*. It does not come from the reality that a true state of emergency exists.

To resist manipulation, you need to alter your *reaction* to your own negative feelings. The fact is that the anxiety, fear, and guilt manipulators so effectively play on will *not* cause you to self-destruct if you fail to quash them immediately. They certainly will cause you discomfort. But discomfort *can* be tolerated and withstood. In fact, the longer you allow yourself to stay exposed to the uncomfortable feelings, the more likely it becomes that your discomfort actually will decline in intensity. Psychologists call this phenomenon *habituation*.

However, in order for your fear, anxiety, or guilt to habituate—that is, to decrease in intensity—you must overcome the impulse to jump through the white door in order to gain temporary relief. Remember, each time you react to your feelings of fear, anxiety, or guilt by acquiescing to the manipulator's demands, you fuel the manipulative cycle.

As you train yourself to withstand the discomfort so that you can make the positive, healthy changes in your behavior, your tolerance will increase. Instead of panicking or overreacting to the negative feelings the manipulator creates, relabel the discomfort you feel as a necessary and worthwhile price to pay to make constructive changes in your life.

There is another reason to change your panicky, urgent reactions to negative feelings. Urgency can produce a thinking error called *emotional reasoning*. This happens when you confuse your negative feelings with the thought or belief that something negative or bad is actually happening or is going to happen. And the stronger and more overwhelming the bad feelings are, the more spillover there is likely to be from your emotions to your thought process.

Just because you are afraid of a manipulator's anger, for example, does not necessarily mean that something dire is really about to happen. The manipulator likely will get over his anger, and you will tolerate the fear, especially with the help of the following desensitization technique. Or just because you feel guilty for not acquiescing immediately to a manipulative family member's demand, it does not necessarily follow that your relationship with that person will be damaged inalterably or that you will lose their love.

Lowering the urgency with which you react to negative feelings *and* decreasing the intensity of those feelings will have a corrective effect on the emotional reasoning that fuels the manipulative cycle.

You will not need to use sheer willpower to change your reactions to fear, anxiety, and guilt. Instead, you will be bolstered with the benefit of a potent psychological technique called *desensitization*. Here is how it works:

The basic principle of desensitization is that you cannot feel relaxed at the same time that you feel fearful, anxious, or guilty. This, you will agree, seems logical on its face. Thus, by using behavioral conditioning, you will assume a state of relaxation with the help of a deep-breathing exercise while you simultaneously recall an actual experience in which the manipulator elicited strong negative emotional reactions in you.

To accomplish the conditioning, you need to recall at least three (more is fine) situations in which you experienced fear, anxiety, and/or guilt as a result of the manipulator's actions and therefore felt pressured to comply with the manipulator's desires. Use examples that are quite vivid in your memory. Write down a sketch of each example, taking care to describe just what the manipulator said or did that made you feel the uncomfortable emotions. Also describe your reaction of fear, anxiety, and guilt in as much detail as possible.

Next, using a cassette recorder equipped with a microphone, record a tape of your three examples simply by reading your written descriptions. Of course, any embellishment or elaboration you add is even better. No one will listen to the tape except you. Your purpose here is to recreate the experience of anxiety, fear, or guilt.

Here is how you put the components of desensitization together: Lie down on a comfortable bed or sofa. Have your cassette player and the tape you made ready by your side. Begin by breathing deeply through your nose, wait for a second or two at the top of your inhaled breath, and then exhale fully through your mouth. Continue breathing slowly and rhythmically. Many people find it helpful to visualize a wave washing onto the shore and then returning with the tide back to the sea as they continue their deep breathing.

While you are breathing, focus your attention on your arms and legs. As you continue to breathe deeply, focus on this thought: "My arms and legs are growing heavy and warm." Focus on how heavy your limbs feel as they sink deeper and deeper into the cushion of your bed or sofa.

After 2 to 3 minutes of relaxation breathing, you are ready to turn on your tape recorder. Continue to breath and to relax your body as you listen to the first recollection that you have recorded. In your mind's eye, visualize as clearly as possible the scene that is being described. As you listen to yourself describing the negative emotional reactions, put yourself in the scene, and try to experience those same feelings.

Now the key to desensitization is to maintain as much physiologic relaxation as you can while simultaneously visualizing the scene in which negative emotions were aroused. As you allow yourself to feel anxiety, fear, or guilt, be conscious of how you are able to control the feelings by maintaining your deep breathing and the relaxation of your body.

As the tape of your first description ends, turn off the tape recorder. Keep the visualized scene clearly in your mind. Try to really feel the negative emotion(s) being conjured in your memory. Focus again on your rhythmic breathing. Now say to yourself, "I may be feeling anxious or afraid or guilty, but I *can* tolerate it. I am okay." Continue breathing deeply and letting your limbs feel heavy and warm.

Repeat the exercise for the other two examples you have recorded. Each time, notice that you can counter the discomfort of fear, anxiety, or guilt by refocusing on your relaxation breathing and passive muscle release.

Practice the exercise of combining relaxation as you visualize your recollections at least twice each day for a week or two. Every time that you practice, it will become easier to accomplish the pairing of your negative feelings with your counterresponse of relaxation. The more facile you become at the desensitization work, the more effective the technique will be when the first real opportunity for resistance presents itself.

In the actual setting of manipulation, desensitization is a quiet but nevertheless potent tactic of resistance. When the manipulator in your life ratchets up the pressure and seeks to create those now-familiar feelings of anxiety, fear, or guilt, you will resist by immediately thinking, "I am feeling fear (or anxiety or guilt), but I *can* tolerate it. I am okay." And you will recall the feelings of relaxation as you regulate your breathing in a quiet emulation of the deep-breathing exercise.

The resistance comes from what you will *not* do: You will not rush to capitulate or comply with the manipulator's demands because your urgent habit to quash the bad feelings has been broken. You will simply withstand the negative feelings that will decrease in intensity because of the desensitization training that you have practiced and the natural process of habituation.

Step 4: Labeling the Manipulation

As long as the silent contact between you and the manipulator remains in tact, the power of the manipulation will as well. However, when you disrupt the collusion and reveal the hidden agenda by clearly and directly labeling the interaction as a manipulation, the power balance will realign in your direction.

The essence of this resistance is for you to describe in direct language exactly what the manipulator is doing. By describing the manipulation *out loud,* you will go a long way toward disrupting and ultimately foiling the manipulator's purposes. Think of direct, clear communication—especially when it is about the manipulation itself—as the psychological equivalent to holding up a cross to a vampire. Most manipulators recoil in the face of being "busted," and the air goes out of the pressure they are trying to create just as easily as it escapes a punctured balloon.

Before you are ready to label the manipulation in the presence of the manipulator, you will require some preparation and, again, some practice. Begin by selecting an example from recent memory. You may use one of the same examples from the desensitization exercise or any other instance when the manipulator has coerced you into compliance.

The best way to analyze the manipulation is to use what I refer to with my patients as the "ABCD formula." This model will help you to identify the connections between the manipulator's tactics and your feelings. Importantly, it points to and articulates an alternative to the current manipulative tactic.

Think back to your example of a time when you were manipulated and fill in the blanks in the following sentences:

> [**Behavior A**] "When you do [describe what the manipulator does that you find unpleasant, hurtful, or uncomfortable],
> [**Emotion B**] I feel [state the emotion you feel].
> [**Alternative behavior C**] If you would stop doing [behavior A] and if you would instead do [describe an alternative nonmanipulative behavior],
> [**Emotion D**] I would feel [state your desired emotion]."

Here is an example from the analysis of one of my patients who had a highly manipulative husband. Here is what she said to him:

[A] "When you raise your voice and yell at me,

[B] I feel afraid and anxious.

[C] If you would just stop yelling and ask me what you want in a calm voice,

[D] I would feel a lot more respected and valued."

Ask a supportive friend, therapist, or other person to assist you by role-playing your resistance. Set up the scenario and ask the other person to behave like the manipulator. Ask the other person to do or say what the manipulator typically does. Then it is your turn to resist by *labeling the manipulation.*

Using the ABCD model, lay out the manipulative behavior, your reaction, the alternative preferred behavior, and your reaction to the alternative. Pay particular attention to the wording of the emotional statements. By using the form "I feel [emotion]" instead of "You make me feel [emotion]," you are taking responsibility for your own feelings rather than blaming the manipulator. And while you may feel strongly that the manipulator, in fact, *is* responsible for making you feel bad, laying the blame on another person for your feelings is really the manipulator's style rather than yours. The recommended form is far more effective.

Practice keeping your voice relatively quiet and low in volume. Your goal is to project quiet strength; yelling is for manipulators. Stick with the ABCD formula. You do not need to explain or say anything more. Remember, this resistance step is merely to label the manipulation.

You will need to learn one final statement to conclude this step. Return to behavior A, and state in a direct, nonprovocative or nonaccusatory way, "I understand that it is your choice to [engage in behavior A]. Now you know how I feel when you [engage in behavior A]."

In a sense, this closing statement gives the manipulator the benefit of the doubt. Just in case you have not explained your emotional reactions to his manipulations or on the outside chance that the manipulator does not really know how his behavior is affecting you, this statement puts to rest those excuses.

Once you have labeled the manipulation and informed the manipulator of your feelings, the ball is back in his court. Now, if the manipulator's toxic behavior persists, you can conclude that his intention is to cause you to feel the uncomfortable emotions that previously have propelled you into capitulation.

When you have practiced sufficiently, you will be ready to resist by labeling the manipulation next time the manipulator pulls out his or her pressure tactics. And you will be ready for the next key resistance step.

Step 5: Disabling the Manipulation

This resistance step holds the key to your freedom. You will tell the manipulator from a position of quiet strength that her tactics will no longer work to accomplish her purposes.

Return to your examples from the last few exercises. Identify a specific goal that the manipulator has pursued with you. What did the manipulator want you to do or say? If you cannot define a specific goal, you can use a generic version (see below). Use the manipulator's goal to fill in the following sentence: "I understand that you want me to [manipulator's specific goal]" or "I understand that you wish I would do what you want [generic/nonspecific]."

Now review the following list, and circle all the tactics that the manipulator typically uses to get her way. Add more if necessary.

Silent treatment
Yelling/screaming/raising voice
Swearing
Name-calling
Door slamming
Fist pounding
Angry facial expressions
Laughing
Crying
Sulking
Pouting
Criticizing
Sighing
Ignoring
Threats
Negative predictions

To disable the manipulation, you need to state that you understand the manipulator's goal but that the manipulative tactic she is choosing to use will not work to accomplish that goal.

Here are some examples of how this resistance tactic sounds:

"I understand that you want me to do this work for you, but your threats are not going to be effective any longer."

"I understand that you want me to go with you tomorrow, but giving me the silent treatment and ignoring me is not going to be effective."

"I understand that you wish I would do what you want, but your anger, swearing, and fist pounding are not going to work on me anymore."

The best way to practice is to combine steps 4 and 5. You can readily see that the two resistance steps used in combination are like a one-two punch. You will tell the manipulator that you now know exactly what she is doing *and*, importantly, how you feel in reaction to her tactics. Then you will simply inform the manipulator that although you understand what she wants of you, the old tactics will no longer work to coerce your compliance.

Step 6: Setting Your Terms

As you implement the resistance tactics, you will experience the reemergence of your identity. By recalibrating the power balance and effectively holding off the manipulator's coercive tactics, you will be establishing new personal boundaries.

This step of resistance will make those boundaries explicit. Here is where you communicate clearly and directly that you will no longer participate or collude in being manipulated. The components of this resistance step are:

1. Announce your intention to make your own decisions about what you will or will not do in the relationship based on taking your own needs and interests into account along with those of other people (including the manipulator).
2. Teach the manipulator how you want to be treated—for example, with respect, as a person of value and integrity, as an adult or equal partner. Communicate directly that you will not allow yourself to be hurt.
3. Establish clear boundaries and limits. Give notice that manipulative tactics are no longer acceptable (e.g., no more silent treatment, no guilt trips, no intimidation through anger or threats of abandonment). Do not

threaten. Just make it clear that you will not participate in any conversation that includes the off-limits
tactics.

4. Ask the manipulator to acknowledge that you have
needs, values, opinions, and preferences for your own
behavior that, while they may be *different* from his
or hers, they are *not* bad or wrong.

5. Tell the manipulator that you are hopeful that by setting limits and reestablishing your personal integrity,
the overall quality of the relationship for both of you
will improve.

Naturally, you should practice making these statements,
ideally through role-playing. Make each point directly and
with a minimum of elaboration or explanation. This is your
personal emancipation proclamation.

Of course, it is unlikely that the manipulator will comply
with an automatic, "Oh, sure." However, if you have used
some or all of the resistance tactics discussed earlier, the
manipulator will not really be surprised. In a sense, you are
just telling him directly what you have already been displaying with your newly found abilities to resist the manipulative
control.

You may feel quite anxious about making these statements.
Do not allow your anxiety to dissuade you. You should be
even more anxious and fearful about continuing to lose yourself—your values, independence, and integrity—by allowing
yourself to be stifled and subjugated by a manipulative con-
troller.

What you certainly can and ought to expect is fallout.
Initially, the manipulator may respond by turning up the pressure and coercion several degrees. You must not succumb

now. Use your broken-record skills to reiterate your statement of terms. If she is going to come around to a healthier, happier relationship, you will see it happen in response to your strength, not to your weakness.

You must face the possibility that the manipulator may not wish to continue the relationship under any terms but her own. And you are wise to confront this possibility right now. In a very real sense, the statement of your terms becomes a litmus test for the value of the relationship in the first place. If you discover that the manipulator's only terms for maintaining the relationship are your continued manipulation and exploitation, you will have some serious decisions to make. Extraction may well be your best and healthiest option.

Naturally, even if the manipulator sees the light and acknowledges a willingness to change, you should not expect the relationship to self-correct overnight. The manipulator will need time to learn new ways of behaving and better ways to ask for what he wants. However, your patience, consistency, and resoluteness are the orders of the new day.

Step 7: Compromising and Negotiating

While there is no compromise or negotiation on the tactics used by the manipulator, there needs to be a healthy give and take on meeting your respective needs and preferences. As you will recall, a hard-core manipulator is only interested in serving his own interests and his own ends. Left to his own devices, the manipulator will not automatically be looking out for what you need or desire.

However, if the manipulator is ready to accommodate and adapt to the healthy changes that you have initiated, there is room for both of your interests to be served. This final resistance step shows you the basic model of conflict resolution through compromise and negotiation.

I am using the term *conflict* here not to mean an argument or full-blown confrontation, although mishandled conflict often can escalate to just that. In this context, *conflict* simply means that you and the (former) manipulator have different preferences or desires concerning interdependent decisions or things that involve or affect both of you or require both of you to coordinate your actions.

Since the manipulator is no longer able to get his way by making unilateral demands and turning up the pressure to force your compliance, new, more constructive methods are required. Here are the basic steps to negotiate a compromise or joint solution to a conflict of interest, preference, or values:

1. Describe the other person's position in clear, unambiguous terms: "I understand that you want/would like/would prefer _____."
2. Confirm your understanding of his position. Ask him to clarify as necessary.
3. State your position or preference directly in clear, unambiguous terms: "I would like/prefer _____."
4. Allow for and directly answer questions designed to clarify both positions, especially with respect to how each of you feels about the alternatives and about the degree of importance attached to the issue.
5. Enlist the (former) manipulator in a search for a compromise: "Is there a third alternative that might work for both of us? Let's try to think of one."

6. Or enlist the (former) manipulator in a fair but random choice solution. "Since we can't agree, let's flip a coin. We'll do it the way the winner of the coin toss wants."

7. Or enlist the (former) manipulator in an exchange, barter, or turn-taking solution: "I'll do _____ for you if you'll do _____ for me" or "We'll do it my way this time and your way next time (or vice versa)."

The essential point here is that compromise and negotiation are possible.

This final resistance step is really a wholesale substitute for manipulation. There is simply no room for manipulative tactics in your newly defined relationship. When both parties are heard and understood, and when their desire to reach solutions that advance the welfare of the relationship instead of each individual is paramount, the manipulative cycle is finished.

Many of my patients over the years have come to me trapped in what they initially felt were relationships with intractable manipulators. Many have had success in getting the former manipulator in their lives to compromise and negotiate. However, they first learned how to choose their battles.

Choosing Your Battles

The preceding tactics will allow you to launch a full-scale resistance that will end manipulation and let you reclaim control over your own life. However, you must choose your battles carefully and wisely.

Use the steps selectively, and assess the manipulator's responses. Some manipulative relationships do change and become far more positive and healthier in character. Sadly, though, some—maybe even most—do not. You may use the steps as a kind of test evaluation to determine whether your manipulative relationship has the flexibility and strength to transform.

You know the circumstances and complexities of your particular relationship. Many factors may enter into your decision to stay or leave, resist or submit, or settle for limiting the damage and improving the situation as opposed to full-scale recovery and change.

If you are being manipulated at work, for example, your resistance may require a small-scale, carefully orchestrated campaign that will help to improve the way you feel about yourself while protecting your job and your livelihood. You may never choose to confront a controlling and potentially irrational boss. However, taking back control in small ways and looking for an alternative to your current employment situation may be sufficient to lower your current stress and allow you to preserve your self-esteem while you gradually and safely put your liberation plan into action.

Or, like a former patient, you may abandon small-scale steps for personal revolution. He was a vice president at a large public relations firm in Los Angeles. He was earning a lot of money but was unhappy with his work surroundings, due mainly to his boss. When he first came to see me, he would not have labeled his negative work experiences as his having been manipulated, but gradually he came to see how his boss' manipulative work style and lack of work ethic was affecting him. One morning, as he was riding the escalator up from the underground garage into the high-rise office lobby, a uniformed security guard, who was stationed at the top of the stairs, looked at him and said, "I don't think I've ever seen anyone look unhappier than you." This comment came from a total stranger! My patient rode the elevator to his office on the thirty-first floor and immediately made plans to extract himself from that painful environment. Two weeks later, he walked into the president's office and gave his notice. He felt better the minute he had determined what he was going to do and great relief when he resigned. He has never regretted that decision.

Whether you employ small-scale resistances or cause a personal revolution, you now understand the damage that manipulation can cause to your emotional and physical health if you make no changes at all and allow your victimization to persist. You are now empowered to get out from under the manipulative control that is making you unhappy. You know how to resist. Choosing how, when, and with whom is up to you.

13

How to Make Yourself a Hardened Target

EARLIER IN THIS BOOK you learned that certain flawed ways of thinking—especially about yourself in relationship to other people—set you up as an easy mark for manipulators. In Chapter 2 you had an opportunity to measure your own vulnerability and to determine how soft or easy a target you represent to would-be manipulators.

You also have learned that becoming the victim of manipulation *creates* points of vulnerability. By allowing another person to pull your strings, you become less self-reliant and less inclined to see yourself as the prime mover of your own life. As a consequence, your self-esteem drops, your sense of identity blurs, and your internal focus on what constitutes your core self becomes fuzzy and obscure.

If you have people-pleasing tendencies, approval addiction, anger phobia, and/or assertiveness problems, these buttons get pushed repeatedly by manipulators and therefore become more deeply ingrained as your collusion with manipulation persists.

In short, the areas of vulnerability that make you a soft target are both the cause *and* the consequence of becoming enmeshed in one or more manipulative relationships.

If you have started implementing the resistance tactics, you are on your way to extricating yourself from manipulative control. By changing your behavior, you have started the process of correcting the self-defeating thoughts and beliefs that have made you an easy mark.

Now it is time to launch a direct attack on those thought patterns and, in so doing, to transform yourself into a hardened target instead of a soft one. As a result of the difficult and painful experiences you have endured in manipulative relationships, you should be highly motivated to change. You understand far better than ever before how dangerous—to both your emotional and physical well-being—it would be to hang onto the kind of thinking that will just lead you into another manipulative trap.

Altering your thinking is yet another pathway to achieve more far-reaching, constructive changes in your feelings and your behavior. Psychologically, your thinking, behavior, and feelings are linked together in a kind of delicate balance. People find it very unpleasant when one part of the system is out of sync or is incongruous with another. The technical term for this imbalance is *cognitive dissonance*. Consider it a conflict between *any two* of the three mental elements—your thinking, behavior, or feelings.

Because of the clash it creates in our mind, we generally do not like to act one way and think or feel another. When this happens, we feel phony, disingenuous, or just downright confused. The dissonance or discomfort motivates us to get the system back in balance by realigning the parts and making them fit together harmoniously.

When it comes to being manipulated, vulnerable thinking supports victimized behavior and the negative feelings that come along with both. By implementing the resistance tactics, you are using the leverage of dissonance to modify your thoughts and feelings. In other words, by *acting* as someone who will no longer submit to manipulation, you lead your thinking and feelings to change in nonvictimized, healthier directions. Remember the admonition: *Change your behavior, and your mind (i.e., your thoughts and feelings) will follow.*

In very much the same way, correcting flawed thoughts and beliefs will have a healthy effect on your actions and emotions. Thus, by *thinking* like a hardened target, you will become one.

You have tasted the bitter pill of manipulation. Now you are ready for a healthy dose of *cognitive therapy*—a proven method for correcting the flawed, erroneous thinking that propels capitulation to manipulators.

Cleaning the Bugs in Your Mental Computer

The self-defeating thoughts and beliefs that make you vulnerable to manipulation are like a virus that has infected your mental hard drive. To rid yourself of that virus and harden yourself to manipulators, you will follow three basic steps, which I will explain below:

1. Record your "automatic," unedited, and uncensored thoughts in a written journal.
2. Scan your stream of thoughts to identify *all* soft-target beliefs and attitudes.

3. Replace each soft-target thought or bug with a corrected hard-target statement.

Cognitive therapy teaches you to develop a keen examiner's perspective on your own thought process. Psychologists have long observed that merely by asking patients to write down their "automatic" or unedited thinking, the process of change is set into motion. This is so because writing down your thoughts greatly increases your awareness of what is going on in your own mind.

By perusing your thoughts with a sharp eye toward detecting soft-target errors, you will develop insight into how wrong-headed thinking has made you an unwitting collaborator of manipulators. Finally, by replacing the flawed thoughts with healthier, self-protective ones, you will gain far better control over the moods and emotions that thinking creates. Most important, of course, you will have steeled yourself as a hardened target to future manipulators.

Collecting Your Thoughts in a Journal

In order to debug your mental computer, you will need to sample its contents on a regular basis. The more samples you have of your thinking, the more effective your target-hardening efforts will be.

You should focus on the relationships in your life that you find most difficult or problematic. The trigger for making a journal entry is any situation or interaction with another person that creates uncomfortable or unpleasant feelings for you. Your emotional triggers may include anxiety, fear, guilt, obligation, confusion, sadness, anger, disappointment, or any other feeling that you experience as negative. Certainly you should make a journal entry anytime you feel manipulated.

Try to write down your thoughts as soon after the situation or incident as possible. Jotting down some quick notes immediately will aid your recall in case you cannot get to your journal for several hours.

Your journal entry should include the date, time, and a brief description of the situation or problem that has occurred. Include a description of your feelings. The key is what comes next: You must write down your thoughts as though you were taking dictation from your mind directly onto the journal paper.

It is imperative that you record your "automatic" thinking without editing, censoring, or changing what has appeared naturally in your stream of thought. Record your thoughts about the situation, your relationship with the other person(s), and your emotional reactions.

Since you are trying to uncover soft-target thinking that makes you vulnerable to manipulation, you should use the following list of the seven emotional buttons—or areas of vulnerability—as prompts or cues. Write down your automatic thinking about:

- Your people-pleasing habits and mind-sets
- Your need for approval and acceptance; and your need to avoid rejection, criticism, and abandonment
- Your fear and avoidance of anger, conflict, and confrontation
- Your inability to say no
- Your blurred sense of identity
- Your low self-reliance

- Your external locus of control—Your tendency to see others as most responsible for what happens to you.

How to Recognize Soft-Target Thinking

Before you scan your journal for evidence of flawed thinking, you need to spend a bit of time doing some homework. Homework, by the way, is an integral part of cognitive therapy.

Your assignment is to learn to recognize soft-target thinking and to understand how and why it makes you vulnerable to manipulation. To help you, I have provided several examples of soft-target beliefs in each of the seven areas of vulnerability.

The soft-target examples I have provided are not intended as an inclusive list that covers every person's unique or precise thoughts. That, of course, would be unfeasible. Rather, the examples are designed to give you a good working sense of the style, type, and content of thinking that is self-defeating because it opens the door to manipulators.

I recommend that you read each example out loud. Ask yourself if you recognize this *type* of thinking—allowing for variations in wording and different versions of expression—in your own thought process. If your instinct is to agree with any of the soft-target statements, you have identified a flaw in your thinking. (Look back at your answers to the quiz in Chapter 2. Your score is the number of soft-target statements out of a maximum of 40 with which you agreed.)

As you read each soft-target example in the following subsections, try to assume the perspective of a manipulator. What is it about this kind of thinking that attracts the attention and interest of manipulators? How would a manipulator exploit this kind of thinking to his or her advantage? How would she push your buttons?

People-Pleasing Habits and Mind-Sets

This kind of thinking—and the behavior that it promotes and supports—is contaminated and distorted by self-sabotaging *should* statements about yourself and other people. If you subscribe to people-pleasing beliefs, your self-esteem is overly attached to how much you do for others and how successful you are at pleasing them. As a result, you take care of everyone else's needs at the expense of your own. The price you pay for being *nice*—a personality trait central to your identity—is that other people will manipulate and exploit your willingness to please them.

Here are some examples of people-pleasing thinking that set you up to be a soft-target for manipulators:

PEOPLE-PLEASING SHOULDS

1. I *should* always do what others want, expect, or need from me.
2. I *should* always put other people's needs first, before my own.
3. I *should* always try to please other people and make them happy.
4. I *should* never say no to anyone who needs me or disappoint anyone in any way.
5. I *should* always be nice even if I feel angry or upset inside.
6. Other people *should* like and accept me because of how hard I work to please them.
7. Other people *should* appreciate and love me because of all the nice things I do for them.

8. Other people *should* never reject or criticize me because I always try to live up to their expectations.
9. Other people *should* not be angry with me because I would go to any length to avoid conflict, anger, or confrontation with them.
10. Other people *should* be kind and caring to me in return for how well I treat them.

THE NEED TO BE NICE

1. I pride myself on being a nice person.
2. I believe that I should always be nice even if it means allowing others to take advantage of my good nature.
3. I try to make other people like me by being a nice person.
4. I want everyone to think of me as a nice person.
5. Being nice often prevents me from expressing negative feelings toward others.

PUTTING OTHERS FIRST

1. I always try to meet the needs of others, even at the expense of my own needs and desires.
2. If I stopped putting others' needs ahead of my own, I would become a selfish person, and other people would not like me.
3. I would feel guilty if I did not make the needs of others more important than my own.
4. I expect to give more in relationships than I expect to get back.
5. I often feel that others expect too much from me, but I always try not to disappoint them or let them down.

You Are What You Do

1. I believe my value depends on the things I do for other people.
2. I rarely delegate tasks to others.
3. I believe that other people like me because of all the things I do for them.
4. I would think of myself as a bad or selfish person if I did not always try to give of myself to those around me.
5. I feel that I need to prove myself to others by doing nice things to make them happy.

Approval Addiction

There is nothing wrong or unhealthy about valuing the approval of others, especially those you love and respect. However, when your need to have *everyone's* approval—and to avoid their disapproval—becomes imperative for your emotional survival, you have moved into the dangerous soft-target zone.

If you are an approval addict, your behavior will be as easy to manipulate and control as that of any other junkie. All a manipulator needs to do is to give you the approval you crave and then simply threaten to take it away if you do not comply.

Here are some examples of soft-target approval-addiction beliefs:

1. It is extremely important to me to be liked by nearly everyone in my life.
2. I have always needed the approval of other people.
3. When someone criticizes me, I get very upset.

4. I need others to approve of me in order to really feel worthwhile and happy.

5. My self-esteem depends greatly on what other people think of me.

Fear of Anger, Conflict, and Confrontation

When this hot button is exposed, a manipulator has an easy job of gaining control over you by using tactics of intimidation to arouse your fear. The manipulator knows that you will comply in order to avoid the eruption of anger, conflict, or confrontation.

Here are some examples of soft-target thinking in this area:

1. I would go to almost any length to avoid a confrontation.

2. I believe that nothing good can come from conflict.

3. I believe that something bad or destructive will result if anger and conflict are expressed in a relationship.

4. I am easily intimidated by another person's display of anger or hostility.

5. I believe that I am usually to blame if someone gets angry with me.

Lack of Assertiveness and Inability to Say No

If you lack the ability to say no to others' needs, requests, or demands, you are a walking bull's-eye for a manipulator. Saying no may make you feel guilty or selfish or mean-spirited because you equate it with disappointing others or letting them down. Or you may fear that saying no will set off another person's anger or start a conflict. Thus, after years of saying yes, you have taught others to expect you to comply and left the door wide open to manipulation.

Here are some examples of soft-target thinking in this area:

1. I often say yes when I would really like to say no to requests from others.
2. When I say no, I feel guilty.
3. I worry that other people will be angry with me if I turn down a request or say no to them in some other way.
4. I am frequently stressed and tired because I have said yes to too many needs of others.
5. It is very difficult for me to ever deny a request from a friend, family member, or coworker.

Blurry Sense of Identity

Having an unclear sense of your own identity—not knowing where you begin and end, whose needs you feel and fill, and what values are central to your core—is a bookend of manipulation. On one side, the lack of clear identity predisposes you to being dominated and controlled in manipulative relationships. And when you become the pawn in other people's power games, the weaker and more blurred your sense of self becomes.

Here are some examples of blurred identity thinking:

1. I have difficulty describing who I really am independent of how other people see me.
2. I do not have a clear sense of myself.
3. I am not sure that I have strong needs or values outside of taking care of other people and making them happy.

4. Sometimes I just feel invisible.
5. I often feel that my identity is absorbed from the beliefs, traits, and values of other people in my life.

Low Self-Reliance

This area of vulnerability goes hand in hand with a blurry identity. If your sense of self is out of focus, your ability to rely on your own judgment will be impaired as well. And if you cannot depend on your own judgment and values to guide your decision making, you necessarily will be prone to overly rely on the judgments and directions of others. Without the ability to act as a reliable counselor to yourself, you are a prime target for manipulation.

Low self-reliance is soft-target thinking that looks and sounds like these examples:

1. I am very insecure and anxious about making decisions on my own.
2. I tend to rely more on the opinions and judgments of others than I do on my own.
3. Without lots of input from others, I just cannot make decisions about big and small matters in my life.
4. I often feel confused by all the feedback I get from others about how to run my life.
5. I do not really trust my own judgment.

External Locus of Control

You have an external locus of control if you believe that the things that happen—or fail to happen—to you in life are more under the control of others than under your own control. In contrast, people who have an internal locus of control believe that the primary source of control over what happens to them in life lies within them.

It stands to reason that if you believe that other people have more influence and control over the outcomes in your life than you do yourself, you will be more vulnerable to their influence and to their attempts at manipulation. And to the extent that you collude with or become victim to their manipulation, your sense of being controlled by forces outside yourself will be reinforced and perpetuated.

Here are some soft-target examples of external locus of control beliefs:

1. I believe that most of the things that happen to me are more in control of other people than within my own control.
2. I believe that luck, opportunity, and the goodwill of others have much more to do with what happens to me than anything that I do by myself.
3. I do not think that there is really very much I can do to prevent or minimize negative things from happening to me.
4. I feel unable to change most of the things in my life.
5. In my relationships with most other people, I believe that I have less control over what happens than they do.

Identify Your Soft-Target Thoughts

Now you are ready to scan your own thought process to detect soft-target beliefs. Carefully examine each of your journal entries. With a colored pen or pencil, underline each statement or phrase that contains soft-target ideas or thoughts. Remember, you are looking for thought content rather than exact wording.

On a separate pad of paper, make a list of the flawed thoughts you have identified. As you list each statement, make a notation of the area of vulnerability (e.g., people-pleasing; low self-reliance; approval addiction, and so on) that the soft-target thought reflects.

Correcting Soft-Target Thinking with Hard-Target Beliefs

To transform yourself into a hardened target that will deter instead of attract manipulators, you will need to replace your flawed thinking with healthier, self-protective ideas. In order to build a solid mind-set of deterrence to manipulation, your hard-target thoughts must be accurate, appropriate, and credible. If you do not find the new way of thinking believable, no one else will either.

Inflated or grandiose statements of your strength and power that you do not really believe will be as flimsy as a house of cards as a protection against manipulators. And replacing your soft-target thoughts with a mantra of repetitive positive affirmations that have no real substance will not work either.

However, when your mind-set is repaired and strengthened with realistic, healthy thinking, it will pose an effective deterrent to manipulators. Most manipulators *will* seek the easiest mark they can find. Your corrected hard-target thinking will create a wall of protection that manipulators likely will find too difficult to breach.

One of my colleagues likens manipulators to opportunistic infections—they are drawn to targets that pose the least resistance or difficulty for them. Since your new and improved thinking will change you from a soft to a hardened target, a manipulator is far more likely to pass you by and search for an easier victim elsewhere.

To help you develop corrective hard-target beliefs, I have provided a number of examples here for all the areas of vulnerability. The "Debugging Guidelines" at the beginning of each section will help you adopt a healthier mind-set as you get ready to clean your mental computer.

How to Correct People-Pleasing Shoulds

Debugging Guidelines: When thinking is contaminated by *shoulds,* it is rigid, inflexible, and extreme. *Appropriate* thinking, on the other hand, is flexible, moderate, and balanced. People-pleasing *shoulds* that dictate rules about your own behavior or about your expectations of others are coercive and controlling. Statements of what you would *prefer* or *like* are far more appropriate. Try using the word *choose* in your corrected thoughts. And soften categorical words such as *always* and *never* with less extreme thinking.

Your self-imposed *should* rules are rigid and nearly impossible to fulfill. Instead of making you happier, they leave you feeling inadequate, disappointed, or angry with others, as well as wide open to manipulation.

Following are some erroneous soft-target thoughts and suggested ways to correct them in order to make you a harder target.

Soft-target thought: "I *should* always do what others want, need, or expect from me."

Corrected hard-target thought: "If and when I want, I can choose to fulfill the wants, needs, or expectations of others who are important to me."

Soft-target thought: "I *should* always try to please other people and make them happy."

Corrected hard-target thought: "I know that it is impossible to please other people all the time or for me to make everyone happy. Setting myself up by trying to do the impossible will only make me feel inadequate and unhappy."

Soft-target thought: "Other people *should* appreciate and love me because of all the nice things I do for them."

Corrected hard-target thought: "I hope that other people love me for the person that I am rather than for what I do for them. When I choose to do nice things for others, I hope they appreciate my efforts."

Soft-target thought: "Other people *should* always like and approve of me because of how hard I work to please them."

Corrected hard-target thought: "I know it is not reasonable or even possible for everyone to *always* like and approve of me. I would like the people whom I like and respect to reciprocate my feelings, but the most important approval I need is my own."

How to Correct the Need to Be Nice

Debugging Guidelines: If you have to compromise your own values, needs, or identity as a special and unique individual, the price of nice is just too high. Being nice will not always protect you from unkind treatment from others. Thinking that it will is likely to make you feel guilty and responsible if others treat you badly. You are under no obligation to reward people who treat you badly or unkindly or who manipulate or exploit you by acting nice and pretending that everything is fine. *It is okay not to be nice* some of the time.

> *Soft-target thought:* "I pride myself on being a *nice* person."
>
> *Corrected hard-target thought:* "I pride myself on being a sincere, honest, genuine, principled, hard-working, and independent [or any other aspect of your self-concept other than the one-dimensional wishy-washy *nice*] person."
>
> *Soft-target thought:* "Being *nice* often prevents me from expressing negative feelings toward others."
>
> *Corrected hard-target thought:* "I realize that sometimes it is far better for me to say what is really on my mind, even if it involves unpleasant feelings, than to stuff my feelings inside and to become depressed, anxious, or unhealthy in other ways just so I can tell myself that I am *nice*."
>
> *Soft-target thought:* "I believe that I *should* always be *nice* even if it means allowing others to manipulate me or to take advantage of my good nature."
>
> *Corrected hard-target thought:* "It is *not* okay for me to let anyone manipulate me. Rewarding people who take advantage of me by being *nice* to them is not only unhealthy, it is also dishonest."

How to Correct Putting Others First

Debugging Guidelines: If you always put others' needs ahead of your own and fail to take proper care of yourself, there is a very good chance that you will wind up being unable to take care of those who matter the most to you. It is entirely possible to care about others *and* to take care of yourself too. There is a big difference between being selfish and acting in your own enlightened self-interest. The latter is a healthy, desirable goal.

You are setting yourself up for manipulation if you fail to teach the people in your life that you have needs, too, and that they bear some responsibility for meeting your needs just as you try—on a selective, appropriate basis—to fulfill theirs. It is *not* always better to give than to receive. In fact, the healthiest relationships involve *both give and take.* Your mistaken belief that you *must* put others' needs ahead of your own *all the time* leaves you wide open to exploitation, coercion, and manipulation.

> *Soft-target thought:* "I always try to meet the needs of others, even at the expense of my own needs and desires."
>
> *Corrected hard-target thought:* "If I continually meet others' needs at the expense of my own, I will wind up feeling stressed, exhausted, and resentful."
>
> *Soft-target thought:* "If I stopped putting others' needs ahead of my own, I would become a selfish person, and other people would not like me."
>
> *Corrected hard-target thought:* "Always putting other people's needs first does not make me a better person; it just makes me a target for manipulators. I need to strike a balance between taking care of myself and selectively taking care of those who are most important in my life."
>
> *Soft-target thought:* "I would feel guilty if I did not make the needs of others more important than my own."

> **Corrected hard-target thought:** "I am not responsible for *everyone's* needs. Since I am not responsible, I have no reason to feel guilty. Playing on my guilt is a tactic of manipulators."

How to Correct "You Are What You Do"

Debugging Guidelines: Measuring your self-worth and defining your identity by how much you do for other people are beliefs that simply beg for a manipulator's exploitation. Healthy relationships are balanced and interdependent. There has to be room for others to do things for you. By shouldering all or most of the burden of needs and responsibilities in your relationships with others, you will bury yourself with stress.

Your compulsion to do more and more *by yourself*—without delegation or adequate support—is a badly flawed formula for building self-worth. In fact, your self-esteem will only be diminished and depleted by the exploitative, manipulative relationships that your flawed beliefs sustain.

> **Soft-target thought:** "I believe my value depends on the things I do for other people."
>
> **Corrected hard-target thought:** "My value as a person depends on far more than just the things I do for other people. While I enjoy doing nice things for others, I really appreciate it when other people do things for me. In fact, my self-esteem suffers when others take advantage of my giving nature through manipulation and exploitation."
>
> **Soft-target thought:** "I believe that other people like me because of all the things I do for them."
>
> **Corrected hard-target thought:** "I want other people to appreciate my efforts to do things for them, but I do

not want them to like me *because* I do so much or to reject me because I may not always be available or willing to help out. I want people to like me for my good qualities, not because I am easily exploited or manipulated."

Soft-target thought: "I rarely delegate tasks to others. I think it is best to do things myself and maintain control of them rather than to rely on others to help me."

Corrected hard-target thought: "I cannot do everything myself. Just trying to do so is the way to lose control, not to maintain it. By allowing myself to always be on the receiving end of delegation, I set myself up as a target for manipulation. Learning to delegate and to say no are key not only to effective stress management but also to protection from people who want to control me."

How to Correct Approval Addiction

Debugging Guidelines: It is simply impossible for you (or anyone else) to get *everyone's* approval *all the time*. So you may as well just stop knocking yourself out trying to do the impossible. Gaining the approval of others may make you feel good—especially if the others are people you like and respect—but you do not *need* the approval of others to validate your worth as a human being.

The most important, effective, and lasting approval is that which you give to yourself. If you have compromised your integrity and autonomy by turning over the strings of control to a manipulator in exchange for his or her approval, you are paying far too high a price.

Soft-target thought: "It is extremely important to me to be liked by nearly everyone in my life."

Corrected hard-target thought: "It is not possible for *everyone* to like and approve of me. After all, I do not really like and approve of everyone else. Gaining the approval of a select group of people whom I love and respect is a more appropriate and attainable goal."

Soft-target thought: "I need others to approve of me in order to really feel worthwhile and happy."

Corrected hard-target thought: "I may like gaining the approval and acceptance of others, but I do not have to have it in order to feel complete, happy, or worthwhile. My sense of value and contentment depends far more on whether *I* approve of the way I am conducting my life than on the elusive approval of others."

Soft-target thought: "I cannot stand it when other people criticize or disapprove of me. It makes me feel worthless, rejected, and like a failure."

Corrected hard-target thought: "I need to be less defensive and fearful of criticism and disapproval from others. My fears make me too vulnerable to manipulation. I know that constructive criticism actually may help me to succeed, but I cannot even hear it because I am so worried about failure. When other people criticize something that I have done, they are not necessarily rejecting or disapproving of me as a person."

How to Correct Fear of Anger, Conflict, and Confrontation

Debugging Guidelines: Your fears of anger, conflict, and confrontation invite manipulators to control you through threats—implicit or explicit—and intimidation. Honest, authentic, healthy relationships permit the *appropriate* expression of occasional anger. Chronic suppression of all anger or conflict is bad for the health of any relationship and harmful to your personal health as well.

A certain degree of conflict is inevitable between people, especially in a close relationship. In fact, conflict is not necessarily a sign of trouble in a relationship, but chronic conflict avoidance is. Constructive conflict aims toward an effective resolution so that the same conflict does not reemerge in the future.

Your fears of negative emotions are only strengthened when you avoid them through compliance, capitulation, suppression, or denial. By gaining experience and learning to handle anger, conflict, and confrontation *constructively* and *appropriately,* you will reduce your vulnerability to manipulation greatly.

> *Soft-target thought:* "I believe that nothing good can come from conflict."
>
> *Corrected hard-target thought:* "Conflict can be quite helpful by increasing communication, building mutual understanding, and forging new agreements that are designed to eliminate its underlying causes."
>
> *Soft-target thought:* "I would go to almost any length to avoid a confrontation."
>
> *Corrected hard-target thought:* "While I really do not like confrontations, I am not willing to give in to manipulation just to avoid one."
>
> *Soft-target thought:* "I am easily intimidated by another person's display of anger or hostility."
>
> *Corrected hard-target thought:* "Although I feel anxious and somewhat afraid when someone displays anger and hostility, I will not let myself be intimidated. Using anger and hostility as a way of pressuring me into

doing something I do not want to do just will not work. I am not to blame if the other person chooses to get angry and hostile. I may not like feeling anxious and afraid, but I *can* tolerate it. Letting myself be manipulated feels a lot worse."

How to Correct Lack of Assertiveness and Inability to Say No

Debugging Guidelines: Saying no assertively and effectively is your first line of defense against manipulation. In addition to protecting you from manipulation, saying no is key to preventing stress, fatigue, and depression as well. You need to say no to *some* people *some* of the time in order to preserve your ability to give to the people that really matter most in your life.

If you feel guilty when you say no, your thinking is infected with an unreasonable *should* rule that makes it your responsibility to comply—to say yes—to anyone and everyone who asks something of you. Corrected thinking points to protecting your emotional and physical well-being by saying no on a selective basis so that you gain control over the stream of demands on your time and energy.

Your value as a human being does *not* depend on the things you do for others. Saying no some of the time to some of the people—especially to manipulators—will in no way diminish your worth in the eyes of others. In fact, your new-found assertiveness likely will enhance it.

> **Soft-target thought:** "I worry that other people will be angry with me if I turn down a request or say no to them in some other way."
>
> **Corrected hard-target thought:** "I cannot possibly say yes to every request or need of others. I have every right

to say no and to be selective about when and on whom I spend my valuable time and energy. I will communicate my denial in a respectful but assertive way. If the other person decides to get angry with me, that is his or her choice."

Soft-target thought: "It is very difficult for me to ever deny a request from a friend, family member, or coworker."

Corrected hard-target thought: "The reason that it is hard for me to deny requests from others is because I do not have much practice doing it. However, as I gain more experience saying no, the less difficult it will become."

Soft-target thought: "When I say no, I feel guilty."

Corrected hard-target thought: "I do not feel guilty saying no because it is *not* my responsibility or obligation to say yes to everyone. It is my responsibility to protect myself from stress and manipulation by learning to assertively say no."

How to Correct a Blurry Sense of Identity

Debugging Guidelines: Allowing your identity to remain out of focus will keep you trapped in a vicious cycle of vulnerability to and victimization by manipulation. Correcting soft-target thinking in this area is a matter of asking and answering self-defining *"Who am I?"* questions.

- *How do I see myself?* Compose a self-concept word picture using 20 nouns, adjectives, or short phrases.
- *What are my personal boundaries?* How are you similar and how are you different from your spouse or romantic partner, members of your family, friends, coworkers, and other significant people in your life? Compare and contrast your needs, personality styles, and character strengths and weaknesses with at least three others.

- *What are my core values?* What moral or ethical principles are most important to you? What political, social, or cultural attitudes do you hold with conviction and/or passion?
- *What are my spiritual beliefs?* What is your religious faith? How would you describe your personal spirituality?
- *With whom am I bonded?* What people or relationships form your strongest emotional attachments? What relationships define your deepest bonds with others?
- *What are my dreams and goals?* What motivates you? What goals give your life a sense of mission or purpose?

Developing and maintaining a clear sense of your identity is a critical deterrent to manipulators. Flawed, soft-target thinking in this area reflects an external focus—on others' needs and what you do to meet them or on other people's values and beliefs. And to the extent that your thoughts convey a confused, unclear, and blurry sense of self, they continue to pose a soft target.

In contrast, hard-target thinking asks and answers self-defining questions. Hard-target thinking aims internally to collect the thoughts and feelings you have about yourself from which a sharper, clearer, and focused identity is forged.

Soft-target thought: "I do not have a clear sense of myself."

Corrected hard-target thought: "I am working on developing a clearer sense of myself by asking and answering "Who am I?" questions."

Soft-target thought: "I have difficulty describing who I really am independent of how other people see me."

Corrected hard-target thought: "While I find it interesting to know how others see me, it is much more important that I am clear on how I see myself. I need to understand what my core beliefs and values are so that I am not overly influenced or manipulated by others."

Soft-target thought: "Sometimes I just feel invisible."

Corrected hard-target thought: "If I have felt invisible, it is because I have not tried hard enough to see myself clearly from the inside out. If I expect other people to respect me, I must clarify where I begin and end and honor my own personal boundaries. I have valid needs of my own other than just to make other people happy."

How to Correct Low Self-Reliance

Debugging Guidelines: Soft-target thinking in this area impairs your ability to rely on your own judgments and experience to make efficient, effective decisions. Your thinking reveals a lack of trust in the quality of your own independent deliberation. Instead of consulting yourself first and foremost, you prefer instead to flood your own decision-making apparatus with voluminous input from others, often with insufficient regard to the relevance, accuracy, or usefulness of the data you collect or the sources from whom they come.

Often, asking too many people for too much advice creates confusion and ambiguity rather than the clarity and certainty you seek. Because you lack confidence in your own ability to sort through and assimilate the input you have so ardently sought, you require further help from others to help you process and make sense out of the largely extraneous data.

It is no wonder, then, that you approach decision making with feelings of anxiety and insecurity or that you suffer from "buyer's remorse" or eleventh-hour changes of heart. You believe, erroneously, that by asking for nearly everyone's advice—about decisions large and small—you will minimize the chances of making a mistake. What you do not realize is that your method *is* the mistake.

Without taking adequate account of your own feelings, judgments, or needs, your decisions—especially as they pertain to important life issues—are simply ill-informed. Compulsively surveying other people about what they would do if they were you is not going to point the way to your best interests. *You* are the best and most important informant of how you feel about your own life. Like it or not, you must learn to rely on your own counsel.

Your low self-reliance and lack of self-direction broadcast your vulnerability to manipulation. Unless you start thinking like a hardened target, your susceptibility to coercive control will not end.

> *Soft-target thought:* "Without lots of input from others, I just cannot make decisions about big and small matters in my life."
>
> *Corrected hard-target thought:* "Getting too much input from too many people is one reason that I have so much trouble making decisions. Instead, I am going to cast my own vote first. Then I will ask a limited number (maximum of three) of people whose opinion and judgment I truly hold in high regard."
>
> *Soft-target thought:* "I do not really trust my own judgment."
>
> *Corrected hard-target thought:* "I will learn to rely on and trust my own judgment because I am the best source of information about me. Other people can only tell me about their own feelings, not about what is best for me. I will listen to others whom I respect, but the

final decision is not going to be a popular vote. It will
be a single, deciding vote—my own."

Soft-target thought: "I tend to rely more on the opinions
and judgments of others than I do on my own."

Corrected hard-target thought: "Depending more on
others' opinions than on my own is a faulty decision-
making process that I learned. The good news is that
I can unlearn it or learn a better model. When I let
other people know how easily influenced I am by their
input, I make myself vulnerable to manipulators who
do not care about my best interests at all."

How to Correct External Locus of Control

Debugging Guidelines: If you adopt a generalized view of life
that what happens to you is far more in the control of other
people than in your own, you can pretty much expect lifelong
victim status in manipulative relationships. It just stands to
reason that if you believe that other people are supposed to
be in control of what happens to you, they will be. You may
as well just hand over the strings to the next available manipulator and let him pull to his heart's content.

Seeing your life outcomes through the prism of an external locus of control has some other drawbacks, too. People
with an external locus of control tend to have lower self-
esteem than those with an internal locus of control. And
when you do not feel like you can be an effective player in
making things happen in your own life, you just will not tend
to make the kind of self-generated effort or display the strong
motivation that can turn a random turn of luck into seized
opportunity.

External locus of control can make you more vulnerable to depression because it creates feelings of *learned helplessness*— the sense that bad things will happen to you and that there is nothing you can do about them. In addition, holding an external locus of control view can even hurt your physical health by creating a "giving up/given up" mind-set that hinders optimal recovery from serious illnesses.

Correcting this soft-target thinking is straightforward: Decide to start seeing the world from the perspective of someone who has an *internal* locus of control. Think and act *as if* you really believe that what you do *can* make a difference—that *you* are a prime mover and shaker in your own life.

To shift into a hard-target internal locus of control mind-set, you do not have to become delusional or imagine that you are in charge of *everything* that happens. However, you do need to look at the things in your life over which you *can* exercise control and—this is key—start doing something about them.

As you alter your thinking in the direction of greater internalized control, you will reap the psychological benefits of a self-fulfilling prophecy. When you saw the world through the lens of soft-target, external locus of control thinking, you accepted that other people had more influence over what happened to you than you did yourself. Then, to the extent that you colluded with your own manipulation by becoming a victim, your belief that outside forces are in control was reinforced and perpetuated.

Now, with corrected hard-target thinking, you will become less subject to the control of manipulators. In a real sense, then, believing has made it so. You now believe that others are not supposed to have more control over you than you do, and your experience as a hard target is supporting and reinforcing your healthier new perspective.

> *Soft-target thought:* "I believe that most of the things that happen to me are more in control of other people than within my own control."
>
> *Corrected hard-target thought:* "While I am not in control of everything that happens to me, I do have a lot of control over how I am doing in life. People will control me if I give them the strings—and I am no longer willing to do that."
>
> *Soft-target thought:* "I believe that luck, opportunity, and the goodwill of others have much more to do with what happens to me than anything that I do by myself."
>
> *Corrected hard-target thought:* "Luck may have a lot to do with what happens, but I believe that what I choose to do will make the difference between turning a good-luck opportunity into real success versus letting the opportunity just pass by."
>
> *Soft-target thought:* "I feel unable to change most things in my life."
>
> *Corrected hard-target thought:* "Instead of focusing on what I cannot change or control, I am going to put my effort into things that I *can* control. Believing that I am helpless makes me feel powerless and depressed. Believing that I can make my own life better—in big ways and small—is motivating and positive."

Replacing Soft-Target Thoughts with Corrected Hard-Target Thoughts

Using the guidelines and examples in the preceding sections, you are now ready to challenge your own soft-target thinking.

You already have underlined and identified the kind of thinking that makes you vulnerable to manipulation. The final step is to replace each of your flawed beliefs with a corrected hard-target thought. You may borrow from the examples already given or, as appropriate, write hard-target thoughts of your own.

After you write each corrected thought, say it out loud. Assume an attitude of quiet strength and confidence as you read aloud your new and improved mind-set. Notice how much less vulnerable each hard-target thought sounds and how much more empowered you feel as you say it.

Maintaining Yourself as a Hardened Target

To reap fully the benefits of the skills you have learned in this chapter, you should repeat the three-step (scan, identify, replace) journal exercise at least weekly. You developed the soft-target thinking over many years; realistically, you cannot expect it to disappear over night. However, if you remain committed to making yourself a hardened target, those old patterns of thought and behavior can and will give way to far healthier, self protective ones.

Maintaining your hard-target mind-set will require vigilance. Backslides and relapses happen, especially when stresses and time pressures overtake your best intentions. Just be patient with yourself, and do not give up. You *can* recover from any backslide. Just take out your journal and begin again to write down your thoughts. If those old bugs have crept back in, you will know what to do to clean up, correct, and strengthen your thinking.

14

Final Curtain on Manipulation in Five Acts

NOW THAT YOU ARE ARMED with the resistance tactics and hard-target thinking that can help to free you from the manipulators in your own life, I thought you would like to know how the people you met in Chapter 2 dealt with their various manipulative dilemmas. As you will see, some of my patients were able to alter the course of their relationships and to effect lasting changes that stopped or considerably reduced the degree of manipulation. Others, however, opted for the path of extraction or leaving the relationship altogether. However, I can assure you that none of my patients looked back with regret on the actions they took to get out from under manipulative control. On the contrary, these real stories of personal liberation marked true turning points in their lives.

Act One: A Tale of Two Cindys

Once he came to therapy, Bob was a very fast learner. And he had the courage to be forthright and candid with me and, most important, with himself. As a physician, he knew that the stress of the relationship with Cindy was making him unwell and that his health and emotional balance depended on making some big changes.

After a few sessions in which we covered the basics of manipulation, Bob recognized himself as a colluder in a negative-reinforcement cycle. He realized that by capitulating, canceling plans, buying gifts, or otherwise giving in to Cindy's displays of emotion—pouting, crying, screaming—he was only fueling the manipulative fire. He was getting reinforced for caving in as soon as Cindy stopped the negative behavior. And he realized that he was reinforcing and rewarding her for her dependent, clingy behavior.

The real turning point for Bob was when he saw himself as pigeon 2—hooked on a pattern of intermittent reinforcement—compulsively trying to get the "old Cindy" with whom he had fallen in love to reappear. Bob realized that every time he saw a glimmer or a transitory reappearance of the "old Cindy," he got a "fix" and was even more addicted to the sick cycle.

Bob asked Cindy to join him in therapy, but she refused. Instead, she continued to blame him for moving her away from her home where she felt safe and secure. In an ironic twist, Cindy accused Bob of being manipulative and of changing into a person she did not even recognize.

This was the opening that Bob needed. He told Cindy that he believed that they were both disillusioned and disappointed with each other. And he told her that he had made a firm decision to end the relationship before they hurt each other any more. After some crying and anger, Cindy agreed.

Bob bought Cindy a plane ticket back to New York and helped her get resettled. And he called her former employer to recommend that they rehire Cindy as the "best conference planner" they ever had.

Cindy left within the week. Bob's stomach pains stopped. Cindy got her old job back. And 10 months later Bob got married to a pediatrician who practices in his building.

Act Two: Dinner at Mom's

Sally came to therapy in her eighth month of pregnancy. We worked together for about a month before she gave birth. During that time, Sally was committed to learning effective resistance techniques to Martha's manipulation and to Jay's passive-aggressive pressure as well.

The breakthrough came about 6 weeks after the baby was born. Sally returned to therapy, and she was ready to put a battle plan into action. In therapy, she realized that her primary loyalty needed to be to her husband and child—to her own family first—and secondarily to her family of origin. She also realized that Jay's parents and his brothers and sisters and their families were vital to her baby daughter as her grandparents, aunts, uncles, and cousins.

Sally recounted that she did not want her daughter to be "cut off" from Jay's family the way that Martha had cut Sally and Susie off from their own father's relatives. Since Martha did not get along with her own in-laws, she decided to punish them by keeping them from ever getting to know their grandchildren. However, Sally realized that she and Susie lost out on valuable family connections.

I suggested that Sally enlist Susie's help as an ally in her battle with Martha's stubbornness. She invited Susie and her family to dinner one night, where she told Susie how important it was that Jay's family be acknowledged and included, especially now that the baby was born.

Susie was totally supportive. She and Sally went over to Martha's one day and told their mother together about the new arrangement. To preserve family traditions, they were happy to go to Martha's two Fridays a month. On the other Fridays, Sally would host the dinner to which Martha and their father were invited, along with Jay's family.

Sally and Susie role-played the resistance tactics together so that they were well prepared for Martha's manipulative antics. When she cried pitifully, they told her that they were sorry she was choosing to see this change as negative but that this was her choice. She could join them at Sally's or stay home with dad. It was completely up to her.

When Martha called Sally a few days later to express her disappointment and anger, Sally labeled the manipulation and disabled it artfully by saying that Martha's guilt induction or attempts to intimidate her with anger and anxiety just would not work anymore. And Sally used the broken record technique to label Martha's emotion while ignoring the content of what she was saying; then she merely repeated the invitation to join the Friday night festivities at her house with their new granddaughter.

Martha did not bend right away. She actually stayed home with her husband for the first four Fridays that Sally hosted the dinner. But Sally kept issuing invitations and refused to buy into Martha's guilt-peddling attempts.

Finally, when Sally's father decided to join in the resistance, Martha succumbed. He said he was going to Sally's whether his wife joined him or not. And he told her that he would not be a party to cutting his new granddaughter off from half of her extended family by ignoring Jay's relatives.

Martha still tries to manipulate. And she gets away with it some of the time. But Sally has become a much harder target. By changing her thinking, Sally has rid herself of the loathsome guilt that fueled the manipulation for so many years.

Friday night dinners are now at Martha's every other week and at Sally's—with various combinations of Jay's parents and siblings—on the alternative weeks. Now Sally is negotiating with Martha to work out a schedule for holidays and special occasions.

Act Three: Location, Location, Location

Once Francine got a handle on Arnie's true character, she had serious second thoughts about trusting him as a partner. Still, Francine was shocked by Arnie's decision when it was time to discuss their formal partnership agreement.

Arnie simply said that now that the 6-month probationary period was over, he simply was not impressed enough with Francine's "intelligence, motivation, or work ethic" to write formal partnership papers. For her trouble, Arnie proposed to pay her a 20 percent fee on any deals that she had worked on that closed within a year. Otherwise, he was "out of the arrangement."

Francine learned a painful lesson in manipulation from Arnie. In hindsight, Francine actually credits her bad experience with Arnie as ending a naive and immature period in which her soft-target, people-pleasing habit and thoughts made her a natural mark for manipulators. She worked diligently to correct her thinking and to harden herself as a target. And she vowed to stay vigilant to manipulators in business as well as in her personal life.

Three months after the bad experience with Arnie, Francine was asked to join a team of highly successful women brokers. She is now one of the highest producers in the company.

Arnie's wife filed for divorce. A year later, he was forced to leave the firm after a sexual harassment lawsuit against him and the firm was settled for $1 million.

Act Four: Terrible Teens

After Cara's terrible Monday following her party, she went into a major funk. She even refused to go to school for 3 days, having developed a stress-related stomachache.

Cara came with her Mom to a few therapy sessions. With great role-modeling on her mother's part, Cara came to realize that these "popular" girls were not the kinds of friends she ever wanted to have. She was able to alter her thinking so that instead of feeling embarrassed and ashamed for being used, she could think of the shame as more appropriate for the girls who had acted so badly.

"Let them feel embarrassed when they see me," Cara said. "I am so over them."

With her parents' support—and their admission of error by enabling Cara to try to "buy" her friendships—Cara shifted her focus. She decided to get very serious about her academic performance because tenth grade counts for college. And she fell in love with volleyball, a sport she had never played until coming to California.

Cara made the varsity volleyball team and became fast friends with her teammates. She realized how her move to California and her entry into hard-core adolescence thrust her into a highly vulnerable state that manipulative people could exploit.

Cara smiles now as she remembers that painful first month at school. "I made lemonade out of lemons," she says proudly. "But I still have to watch out for manipulators."

Act Five: Double Squeeze

When a second Christmas passed without a proposal from Jay, Valerie decided to make a move—out. After some intensive individual therapy, Valerie decided to take control back over her own life. She realized that as long as she lived with Jay without being married, she was caught in the trap of manipulation. Finally, she had reached the point where her fear of continued living in the limbo zone was far greater than her fear of losing the relationship.

Valerie wrote Jay a letter in which she told him her plans to move to her own apartment the next day. She said that her decision was final. She would no longer feel anxious or guilty about wanting to get married and start a family. And she would no longer endure the threat of his anger or be so terrified of his abandonment or rejection.

She told Jay that she loved him and still wanted to marry him. But she knew that he had to work out his own fears. She said that she earnestly hoped that he would do so before she met someone else.

At first Jay was furious and deeply hurt. He told Valerie that her decision was the confirmation and proof he needed that she was not the right woman to marry—that she would just wind up leaving him like his first wife.

Valerie and Jay were separated for 3 months. Jay began calling Valerie and asking to see her after just 2 weeks. However, Valerie held her ground. She said that the only relationship she was interested in with Jay was to be his wife. Otherwise, Valerie said she saw no reason to get back together.

Valerie went through some very painful and lonely periods without Jay. But she learned to tolerate the discomfort rather than capitulate to the "double squeeze" manipulation that Jay's fears produced.

"If Jay really loves me," Valerie told herself each day, "he'll want to marry me. Otherwise, I'm not losing anything but heartbreak and more pain."

Here's the happy ending: Jay proposed on Valerie's next birthday. They got married a month later.

Conclusion

Y OU NOW HAVE THE TACTICS, strategies, and mind-set to stand up to the manipulators in your life. And you know how to make yourself a far harder target for potential manipulators to exploit or control in the future.

You recognize the costly toll that manipulation takes on your emotional well-being, physical health, and relationships with the nonmanipulative people in your life. Hopefully, the distress you feel will spur you to action. Remember, without *your* determination to initiate changes and to take corrective action, the manipulative relationship will remain status quo. After all, why should the manipulator want to change things?

Armed with effective tools and weapons, you have *almost* everything necessary to mount a successful battle against manipulation. The one thing I cannot give you, however, is the critical final ingredient that will transform this book from just another self-help guide that you place on the shelf into a potent training manual that will empower you to take life-changing action.

That critical ingredient is *courage.*

Courage is the spark that will ignite the change process. So you must reach deep inside and find your personal courage. Your freedom depends on it.

Having courage is not the same thing as being unafraid or without anxiety. On the contrary, by acting with courage, you will proceed to do what is required *despite* the fact that you may feel wobbly, somewhat anxious, or perhaps downright scared to death. Feeling nervous about confronting and resisting the manipulators in your life is only natural. The key is to listen to your strengths and let them guide you; do not let your fears determine your fate.

Set your intention to break free of manipulation: Find your courage, use the skills you have learned, and patiently stay the course. Change—especially if it is to be long lasting—will not happen in a day. However, if you remain committed and diligent, you will be successful.

As you close this book, take a few moments to reflect on this thought:

> *If I am not for myself, who will be for me?*
> *If I am only for myself, what am I?*
> *If not now, when?*

HILLEL, TWELFTH CENTURY

Index